C000126893

Secure Maths
Year 5

a primary maths
intervention programme

Pupil Resource Pack

Collins

William Collins' dream of knowledge for all began with the publication of his first book in 1819.
A self-educated mill worker, he not only enriched millions of lives, but also founded a flourishing publishing house. Today, staying true to this spirit, Collins books are packed with inspiration, innovation and practical expertise. They place you at the centre of a world of possibility and give you exactly what you need to explore it.

Collins. Freedom to teach.

An imprint of HarperCollins*Publishers*
The News Building
1 London Bridge Street
London
SE1 9GF

Browse the complete Collins catalogue at
www.collins.co.uk

10 9 8 7 6 5 4 3 2 1

ISBN 978-0-00-822150-8

Bobbie Johns asserts their moral right(s) to be identified as the author of this work.

British Library Cataloguing in Publication Data
A catalogue record for this publication is available from the British Library.

Publishing manager Fiona McGlade
Editor Nina Smith
Project managed by Alissa McWhinnie, QBS Learning
Copyedited by Joan Miller
Proofread by Jo Kemp
Answers checked by Deborah Dobson
Cover design by Amparo Barrera and ink-tank and associates
Cover artwork by Amparo Barrera
Internal design by 2Hoots publishing services
Typesetting by QBS Learning
Illustrations by QBS Learning
Production by Rachel Weaver
Printed and bound by CPI

Contents

Unit 1: Read, write, order and compare numbers to at least 1 000 000 and determine the value of each digit

million	hundred thousand	ten thousand	thousand	hundred	ten	one	
1	2	3	4	5	6	7	numerals
1 000 000	200 000	30 000	4000	500	60	7	value
One million, two hundred and thirty-four thousand, five hundred and sixty-seven 1 000 000 > 200 000 > 30 000 > 4000 > 500 > 60 > 7 > = 1 234 567							words

1. Use the numbers on the place-value cards to write seven-digit numbers.

a) 2 000 000 + 400 000 + 70 000 + 5000 + 100 + 80 + 9 = ⬡

b) 60 000 + 4 + 200 + 90 + 8 000 000 + 700 000 + 3000 = ⬡

c) 70 + 6 + 500 000 + 9000 + 3 000 000 + 400 + 80 000 = ⬡

2. Write these numbers in **numerals**.

a) twenty-one thousand, eight hundred and fifty-six _____

b) three hundred and seventeen thousand, four hundred and one _____

3. Write these numbers in words.

a) 116 782 _____

b) 7 480 324 _____

4. What is the value of the **5** in each of these numbers?

a) 742 560 _____

b) 4 567 890 _____

c) 2 158 986 _____

5. Write these numbers in order, **largest to smallest**.

a) 6 100 365   5 999 999   6 500 005   6 098 135

_____

b) 3 578 326   3 587 632   3 587 362   3 578 263

_____

Unit 1: Read, write, order and compare numbers to at least 1 000 000 and determine the value of each digit

1. Write these additions as seven-digit numbers.

a) $\boxed{4\,000\,000}$ + $\boxed{500\,000}$ + $\boxed{70\,000}$ + $\boxed{2000}$ + $\boxed{600}$ + $\boxed{50}$ + $\boxed{1}$ = $\boxed{}$

b) $\boxed{800\,000}$ + $\boxed{70}$ + $\boxed{30\,000}$ + $\boxed{5\,000\,000}$ + $\boxed{200}$ + $\boxed{6}$ + $\boxed{9000}$ = $\boxed{}$

2. Write these numbers in numerals.

a) three million, four hundred and seventeen thousand, six hundred and eighty _____

b) seven million, ten thousand and forty-nine _____

3. Write these numbers in words.

a) 560 108 _____

b) 4 050 790 _____

4. What is the value of the **3** in each number?

a) 2 367 800 _____

b) 7 832 195 _____

5. Write these numbers in order, **smallest to largest**.

a) 7 275 450   998 756   6 999 890   899 998

_____

b) 745 912   754 921   754 291   745 921

_____

Unit 2: Number and place value

1. Fill in the snakes to complete the number sequences. Write the size of each step at the end of the snake.

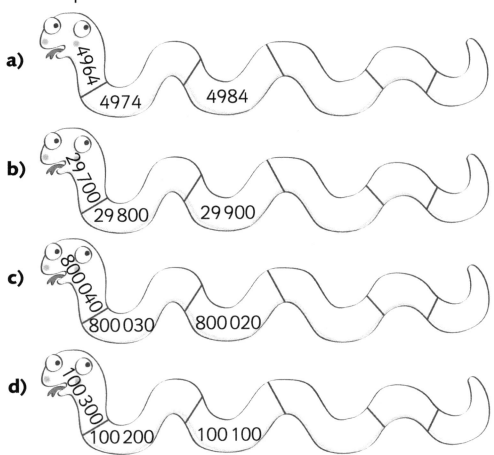

a) 4964 4974 4984

b) 29 700 29 800 29 900

c) 800 040 800 030 800 020

d) 100 300 100 200 100 100

2. Work out which numbers come out of the machines.

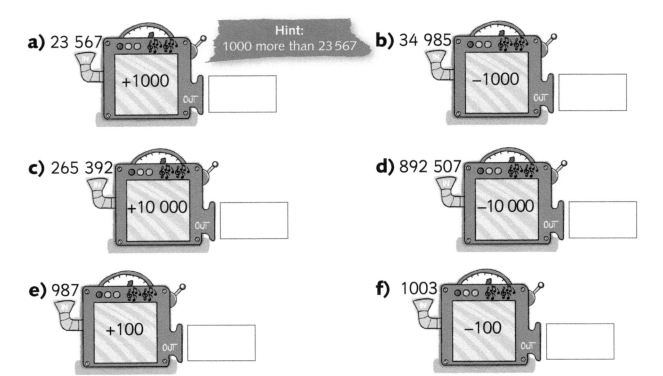

a) 23 567 +1000 OUT

Hint:
1000 more than 23 567

b) 34 985 −1000 OUT

c) 265 392 +10 000 OUT

d) 892 507 −10 000 OUT

e) 987 +100 OUT

f) 1003 −100 OUT

Unit 2: Number and place value

1. In each pair, how much more or less is the second number than the first?

The first one has been done for you.

a) 83 450   84 450   _1000 more_____

b) 712 900   702 900   _____

c) 80 754   79 754   _____

2. Complete each number sequence.

a) 87 490   87 590   87 690   [   ]   [   ]   [   ]

b) 24 875   23 875   22 875   [   ]   [   ]   [   ]

c) 235 600   245 600   255 600   [   ]   [   ]   [   ]

3. Work these out.

a) 23 870 + 1000 = _____

b) 48 921 − 1000 = _____

c) 67 200 + 10 000 = _____

d) 145 892 − 10 000 = _____

4. a) Which number is 1000 **more** than 129 300? _____

b) Which number is 10 000 **less** than 205 650? _____

Unit 3: Interpret negative numbers in context, count forwards and backwards with positive and negative whole numbers, including through zero

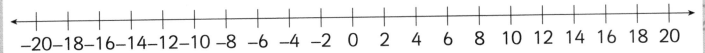

−20 −18 −16 −14 −12 −10 −8 −6 −4 −2 0 2 4 6 8 10 12 14 16 18 20

1. Write the temperature shown on each thermometer.

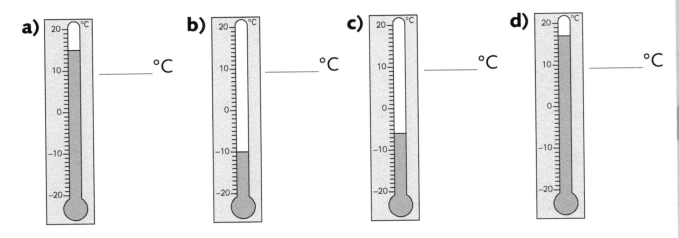

a) _____°C

b) _____°C

c) _____°C

d) _____°C

2. Write the three numbers missing in each sequence.

a) 15 | 10 | 5 | | |

b) | | | −4 | −6 | −8

c) | | | −20 | −30 | −40

d) 7 | 5 | 3 | | |

3. The table shows the average temperature in December for six cities. Use the information in the table to answer the questions.

Moscow: −6°C	Melbourne: 18°C	Lima: 21°C
Tokyo: 8°C	New York: 2°C	Beijing: −1°C

a) Which is the coldest city shown in the table? _____

b) How many degrees warmer is it in Lima than Beijing?
_____ degrees

c) How many degrees cooler is it in Moscow than in Tokyo?
_____ degrees

d) Which city is 16 degrees cooler than Melbourne? _____

Unit 3: Interpret negative numbers in context, count forwards and backwards with positive and negative whole numbers, including through zero

1. Write these numbers in order, **smallest to largest**.

12   –3   –1   0   –9   2

_____

2. Write the next three numbers in each sequence.

a) –20, –15, –10   _____

b) 27, 18, 9   _____

c) 8, 5, 2   _____

3. Write down the last number you will count on the number line when you:

a) Count back 5 from 2.   _____

b) Count on 10 from –3.   _____

4. Use the information in the table to answer the questions.

Average January temperatures

Oslo: –4°C	Cape Town: 28°C
St Petersburg: –6°C	London: 7°C

a) Which is the coolest city shown in the table? _____

b) How many degrees cooler is it in Oslo than in London?

_____ degrees

c) What is the difference in temperature between Oslo and St Petersburg?

_____ degrees

d) How many degrees difference is there between Cape Town and Oslo?

_____ degrees

Unit 4: Round any number up to 1 000 000 to the nearest 10, 100, 1000, 10 000 and 100 000

1. Round these numbers to the number given.

a) 4389 to the nearest 1000 _____

b) 4901 to the nearest 1000 _____

c) 48 643 to the nearest 10 000 _____

d) 42 945 to the nearest 10 000 _____

e) 746 387 to the nearest 100 000 _____

f) 751 735 to the nearest 100 000 _____

2. Complete the table of populations, from the 2011 census, by rounding to the number at the head of each column. The first one has been done for you.

Town	Population	nearest 10	nearest 100	nearest 1000	nearest 10 000	nearest 100 000
Manchester	510 746	510 750				
Cardiff	335 145					
Aberdeen	195 021					
Gloucester	136 362					
Bath	94 782					

3. Write the letter of each given number in the approximate place on the number line.
The first one has been done for you.

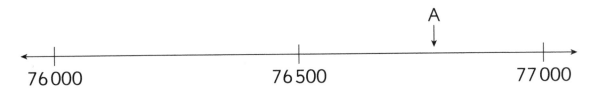

a) A = 76 800

b) B = 76 099

c) C = 76 250

d) D = 76 555

Unit 4: Round any number up to 1 000 000 to the nearest 10, 100, 1000, 10 000 and 100 000

1. Round each number to the number given.

a) 6756 to the nearest 1000 _____

b) 24 509 to the nearest 10 000 _____

c) 765 800 to the nearest 100 000 _____

2. Round 512 945:

a) to the nearest 10 _____

b) to the nearest 100 _____

c) to the nearest 1000 _____

d) to the nearest 10 000 _____

e) to the nearest 100 000. _____

3. Round 99 995:

a) to the nearest 10 _____

b) to the nearest 100 _____

c) to the nearest 1000 _____

d) to the nearest 10 000. _____

4. Draw an arrow to show where the number 45 875 would be on this number line.

```
←———+——————————————+——————————————+——→
   45 800          45 850          45 900
```

Unit 5: Read Roman numerals to 1000 (M) and recognise years written in Roman numerals

1	5	10	50	100	500	1000
I	V	X	L	C	D	M

1. These numbers are written in Roman numerals.
Work out the value of each number.

a) XXXVI _____

b) CCL _____

c) DC _____

d) MMCCCXXV _____

e) MDCXVI _____

f) MMXX _____

2. Write these numbers in Roman numerals.

a) 87 _____

b) 123 _____

c) 258 _____

d) 419 _____

e) 612 _____

f) 895 _____

g) 1364 _____

h) 3999 _____

3. Match the dates, using the diagram to help you.

MCMXC	2010
MMIX	1999
MCMXCV	1990
MMX	2009
MMXIX	2019
MCMXCIX	1995

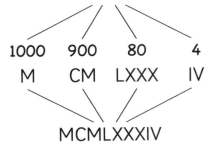

4. What is this date?

VIII.X.MMXVI _____

5. Write your birth date or another important date in Roman numerals.

Write the year in full. _____

_____

Unit 5: Read Roman numerals to 1000 (M) and recognise years written in Roman numerals

1. Here are some numbers written in Roman numerals.
Write each number in figures.

a) XL

b) CXVI

c) DXX

d) MDCCVII

2. Write these numbers in Roman numerals.

a) 75

b) 234

c) 1500

d) 2763

3. Write this date in figures.

XXIV.VI.MCMLXXXII

4. Write 25 December 2015 in Roman numerals.

Unit 6: Solve number problems and practical problems that involve objectives in units 1–5

1. The population figures for these towns and cities are from the 2011 census.

City or town	Population
Birmingham	1 085 810
Newcastle	268 064
Lowestoft	70 945
Aberystwyth	

a) Write the population of each of these cities in words.

Birmingham _____

Newcastle _____

b) Round the population of Lowestoft to the nearest 1000. _____

c) The population of Aberystwyth was eighteen thousand and ninety-three in 2011. Write this number in the table.

d) If the population of Birmingham increased by 10 000, what would its new

population be? _____

e) If the population of Lowestoft decreased by 1000, what would its new

population be? _____

2. Order the cities according to their average low December temperatures, lowest to highest.

Athens 9 °C   Bucharest –3 °C   Glasgow 1 °C   Helsinki –6 °C   Berlin 0 °C

_____

3. Order these dates, **earliest to latest**, according to the Roman numerals, then translate each date underneath.

MDLIX   MMXVIII   MCCXV   MLXVI

_____   _____   _____   _____

_____   _____   _____   _____

Unit 6: Solve number problems and practical problems that involve objectives in units 1–5

1. In the 2011 census the population of Londonderry was **83 125**.

a) Write the population in words. _____

b) Round the population to the nearest 10 people. _____

c) Round the population to the nearest 10 000 people. _____

d) Increase the population by 10 000. _____

e) Decrease the population by 1000. _____

2. Write an approximate number for each letter shown on the number line.

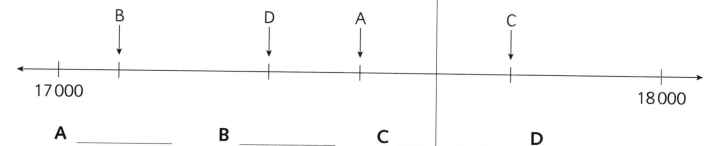

17 000   18 000

A _____   B _____   C _____   D _____

3. Write the number of this year in Roman numerals.

_____

4. Order these temperatures, **highest to lowest**.

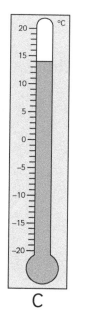

A   B   C   D   E

_____

Unit 7: Add and subtract whole numbers with more than four digits, including using formal written methods (columnar addition and subtraction)

1. Use the grids to work out the addition and subtraction.

a) 132 760 + 609 + 12 599

HTh	TTh	Th	H	T	U
1	3	2	7	6	0
	1	2	5	9	9
+			6	0	9

b) 15 809 – 783

TTh	Th	H	T	U
1	5	8	0	9
–		7	8	3

2. Set out and solve these additions. Use a column method.

a) 25 832 + 28 946

b) 354 901 + 251 783

c) 712 804 + 45 812

d) 14 725 + 999 + 125 936

3. Set out and solve these subtractions. Use a column method.

a) 28 547 – 13 714

b) 54 912 – 9876

c) 8007 – 2858

d) 26 012 – 8745

Unit 7: Add and subtract whole numbers with more than four digits, including using formal written methods (columnar addition and subtraction)

Set out and solve these calculations. Use a column method.

1. a) 27 982 + 25 190

b) 624 094 + 8345

2. a) 54 714 – 23 697

b) 725 348 – 415 639

c) 7002 – 4582

d) 45 115 – 768

3. a) 12 947 + 36 + 5927

b) 29 472 + 33 629 – 47 297

Number – addition and subtraction

Unit 8: Add and subtract numbers mentally with increasingly large numbers

1. Write the output numbers for these function machines.

a) 430, 260, 510, 480

+ 200

b) 780, 460, 590, 370

– 300

_____

c) 1200, 2500, 4300, 5400

+ 4000

d) 4800, 3500, 6700, 1800

– 2000

_____

2. a) Match the complements to 1000.

720 480 540 130 910 50   870 90 950 520 280 460

b) Match the complements to 10 000.

3400 1900 9300 600 4100 7300   9400 2700 6600 5900 8100 700

3. Work out the answers to these problems mentally or with jottings.

a) 345 + 199 = _____

b) 867 – 299 = _____

c) 2364 + 2999 = _____

d) 7726 – 1999 = _____

e) 4725 + 3999 = _____

f) 8293 – 4999 = _____

Unit 8: Add and subtract numbers mentally with increasingly large numbers

1. Write the missing numbers to make the additions and subtractions correct.

a) $640 +$ ⬚ $= 1000$

b) ⬚ $+ 750 = 1000$

c) $7400 +$ ⬚ $= 10\,000$

d) ⬚ $+ 6100 = 10\,000$

2. a) $240 + 500 =$ _____

b) $760 - 300 =$ _____

c) $2500 + 3000 =$ _____

d) $4800 - 4000 =$ _____

e) $3100 + 600 =$ _____

f) $8500 - 200 =$ _____

3. a) $428 + 199 =$ _____

b) $576 - 299 =$ _____

c) $3867 + 2999 =$ _____

d) $9248 - 2999 =$ _____

4. a) $320 + 170 =$ _____

b) $870 - 340 =$ _____

c) $1500 + 2400 =$ _____

d) $6500 - 3100 =$ _____

Unit 9: Use rounding to check answers to calculations and determine, in the context of a problem, levels of accuracy

1. Write each calculation in the correct box. Use rounding to the highest place value.

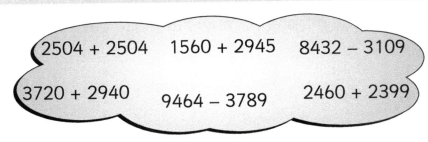

2504 + 2504   1560 + 2945   8432 – 3109

3720 + 2940   9464 – 3789   2460 + 2399

< 5000	> 5000

2. Use estimation to decide whether these **incorrect** answers are too high or too low.

a) 3496 + 2948 = 5444   too _____

b) 7114 – 3293 = 5821   too _____

c) 15 008 + 12 999 – 13 964 = 13 043   too _____

3. Estimate the answer to the calculation by rounding each number to the **nearest thousand**. Draw a line to link the question with the accurate answer, based on your estimated answer. The first question has been answered for you.

Estimated answer	Question	Answers
12 000 + 23 000 = 35 000	12 050 + 22 945	28 680
	34 874 – 6194	31 320
	15 896 + 17 914	34 995
	61 195 – 29 875	29 925
	13 819 + 16 106	33 810

4. Here is list of prices of items bought in an electronics store. Oliver says that the total is less then £1000, Luke says the total is more than £1000. Who is correct? Use rounding to show your working and use this to explain your answer. Do **not** work out the actual total.

£299

£489

£96

Unit 9: Use rounding to check answers to calculations and determine, in the context of a problem, levels of accuracy

1. Round each price to the nearest £10 to find a quick estimate for the total bill.

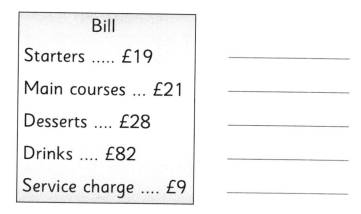

Bill
Starters £19
Main courses ... £21
Desserts £28
Drinks £82
Service charge £9

_____

_____

_____

_____

_____

Estimated total _____

2. Use rounding to estimate the answers to these calculations.

a) $1999 - 965 \approx$ _____   **b)** $5032 + 2895 \approx$ _____

c) $45\,984 - 32\,003 \approx$ _____ $\approx$ means 'is approximately'

3. Use estimation to mark each calculation. Tick (✓) if it is likely to be correct, cross (✗) if it is likely to be incorrect.

a) $16\,109 + 13\,876 = 30\,985$ ☐

b) $30\,925 - 14\,020 = 16\,905$ ☐

c) $19\,156 + 20\,897 - 10\,018 = 29\,035$ ☐

4. Max has saved up £2000 for a school sports trip. These are the costs for the trip. Use rounding to work out if he has saved enough money. You must show your working. Check that you have answered the question.

Accommodation	£1025
Travel	£889
Spending money	£210

_____

_____

Unit 10: Solve addition and subtraction multi-step problems in contexts, deciding which operations and methods to use and why

1. At the beginning of a railway journey there were ⬚54⬚ people on the train. At the first station, ⬚24⬚ got on and ⬚15⬚ left the train. At the second station, ⬚12⬚ got off and ⬚15⬚ got on. How many people are now on the train? Try to work this out mentally.

_____

2. Use the digits   3   9   6   5   1   8   to make:

   a) the largest possible total ⬚⬚⬚ + ⬚⬚⬚

   b) the smallest possible difference. ⬚⬚⬚ − ⬚⬚⬚

3. Charity A has raised £31 490. Charity B has raised £25 765.

   a) Approximately how many **thousands** of pounds has each charity raised?

   Charity A _____   Charity B _____

   b) **Approximately** how much more has Charity A made than Charity B?

   _____

   c) How much more or less is the **exact** difference in amounts and the

   approximate difference? _____

4. A football team's stadium has 70 000 seats. 20 000 of these are sold at a higher ticket price. On one Saturday 17 854 of the higher price seats were filled and 49 018 of the normal price seats. How many spare seats were there? You must show all your calculations.

_____

Unit 10: Solve addition and subtraction multi-step problems in contexts, deciding which operations and methods to use and why

1. Fill in the missing digits.

a)

$$
\begin{array}{r}
2\ \square\ 3\ \square \\
+\ \square\ 9\ \square\ 7 \\
\hline
4\ 5\ 0\ 1
\end{array}
$$

b)

$$
\begin{array}{r}
\square\ 2\ \square\ 5 \\
-\ 4\ \square\ 3\ \square \\
\hline
2\ 3\ 2\ 7
\end{array}
$$

2. The table shows the approximate prices for a return flight from London, UK to Sydney, Australia on a certain date.

Ticket type	Price (£)
Economy	1062
Business	3580
First class	7441

a) How much more or less is the price of **two** business-class tickets compared to the price of **one** first-class ticket?

_____

b) How much more will it cost two people to travel business-class rather than economy?

_____

3. These are the numbers of visitors to a large theme park in the summer months.

June 348 912   July 458 215   August 502 706   September 265 004

How many more visitors were there in **July** and **August** combined than in **June** and **September** combined?

_____

Unit 11: Identify multiples and factors, including finding all factor pairs of a number, and common factors of two numbers

1. Complete the ladders with the next five multiples of the number at the base.

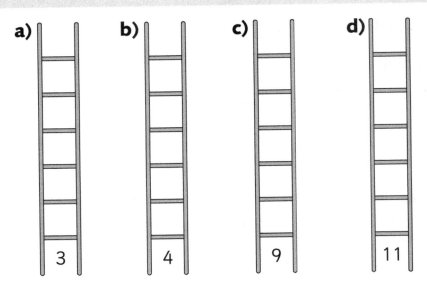

a) 3 b) 4 c) 9 d) 11

2. Write the first 12 multiples of 5. _____

3. a) What is the fifth multiple of 8? _____

b) What is the tenth multiple of 7? _____

4. Complete each factor diagram to show all the factors of the number in the centre, then write out the factors and the factor pairs underneath.

a)

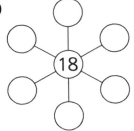

18

Factors of 18: _____

_____

b)

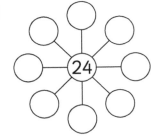

24

Factors of 24: _____

_____

5. Use your answer to question **4** to write down the common factors of 18 and 24.

_____

6. Tick (✓) the box for true or cross (✗) the box for false for each statement.

a) 30 is a multiple of 5. ☐   **b)** 8 is a factor of 30. ☐

c) 4 is a common factor of 28 and 32. ☐

Unit 11: Identify multiples and factors, including finding all factor pairs of a number, and common factors of two numbers

1. Write down the first 10 multiples of 6.

_____

2. a) What is the eighth multiple of 10?

_____

  b) What is the second multiple of 12?

_____

3. a) Write **all** the factors of 10. ____ ____ ____ ____

  b) Write **all** the factors of 30. ____ ____ ____ ____ ____ ____ ____ ____

  c) Write **all** the common factors of 10 and 30. ____ ____ ____ ____

4. Write three factor pairs of 36. ____ × ____, ____ × ____, ____ × ____

5. Tick (✓) the box for true or cross (✗) the box for false for each statement.

  a) 8 is a factor of 28. ☐

  b) 32 is a multiple of 6. ☐

  c) 72 is a multiple of 9. ☐

  d) 8 is a common factor of 24 and 30. ☐

  e) 7 is a common factor of 21 and 35. ☐

Unit 12: Know and use the vocabulary of prime numbers, prime factors and composite (non-prime) numbers

1.

12	4	5	11	18
15	3	7	2	10

  a) Write down the prime numbers from those in the box. _____

  b) Write down the composite numbers from those in the box. _____

2. Work out these mystery numbers.

  a) A prime number between 5 and 10. _____

  b) A composite number < 20 that is a multiple of 9. _____

3. Connect each multiplication to its product.

$2 \times 2 \times 2 \times 5$ 8

3×5 28

$2 \times 2 \times 2$ 40

$2 \times 2 \times 7$ 30

$2 \times 3 \times 5$ 15

4. Write the **numbers** that are **prime** factors of each number.

  a) 12 _____   **b)** 14 _____   **c)** 30 _____

5. Write each number as a product of two prime numbers.

  a) 10 _____ × _____

  b) 21 _____ × _____

  c) 33 _____ × _____

6. Explain why 15 is **not** a prime number.

_____

_____

Unit 12: Know and use the vocabulary of prime numbers, prime factors and composite (non-prime) numbers

1. Write each of these numbers in the correct box below.

1 2 3 4 5 6 7 8 9 10 11 12 13 14 15

Prime number	Composite number	Neither prime nor composite

2. True or false? Tick (✓) or a cross (✗) each statement.

a) 15 is a prime number. ☐

b) 16 is a composite number. ☐

c) 19 is a prime number. ☐

d) 13 is a composite number. ☐

3. Work out the products of prime numbers.

a) 3×5 _____

b) 5×11 _____

c) $2 \times 2 \times 3$ _____

4. Write each number as a product of two prime numbers.

a) 14 _____

b) 35 _____

c) 22 _____

5. Explain why 24 is **not** a prime number.

_____

Unit 13: Establish whether a number up to 100 is prime and recall prime numbers up to 19

1. Work out these mystery numbers.

    a) A prime number between 30 and 35. _____

    b) A composite number between 20 and 30 that is a multiple of both 6 and 8.

    _____

    c) A prime number between 45 and 50. _____

    d) A composite number between 60 and 70 that is a multiple of both 6 and 11.

    _____

    e) A prime factor of 27. _____

2. Write the numbers in the box in the correct places on the Carroll diagram.

2 5 9 18 21 25 22 28 29 30 31 32

	Odd	Even
Prime number		
Composite number		

3. Use the words from the box to fill the gaps to make the sentences true.

prime   composite   multiple   factor   prime factor

    a) 27 is _____ number.

    b) 35 is a _____ of 5.

    c) 5 is a _____ of 40.

    d) 37 is a _____ number.

    e) 8 is a _____ of 40.

Unit 13: Establish whether a number up to 100 is prime and recall prime numbers up to 19

1. There are eight prime numbers between 1 and 20. Write them here.

_____

2. Write each of these numbers under its correct heading in the boxes below.

| 20 | 21 | 23 | 27 | 31 | 33 | 35 | 37 | 39 | 40 |

Prime number	Composite number

3. Complete the sentences.

a) 33 is not prime because _____

_____

b) 43 is a prime number because _____

_____

c) The only even prime number is _____

4. Work out these mystery numbers.

a) The two prime numbers between 15 and 22. _____

b) A composite number between 30 and 40 that is a multiple of 6.

_____

Unit 14: Multiply and divide numbers mentally, drawing upon known facts

1. Connect each number in the middle column to its double and its half.

Double	Number	Half
100	26	19
76	18	9
52	38	25
36	50	13

2. Complete the spider diagram of related facts.

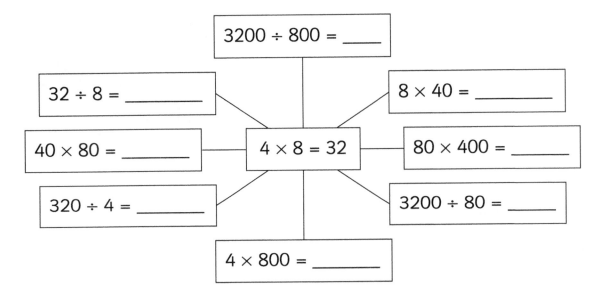

3200 ÷ 800 = _____

32 ÷ 8 = _____

8 × 40 = _____

40 × 80 = _____   4 × 8 = 32   80 × 400 = _____

320 ÷ 4 = _____

3200 ÷ 80 = _____

4 × 800 = _____

3. Use related facts to work these out mentally.

a) 30 × 80 = _____   **b)** 4800 ÷ 60 = _____

4. Write in the missing numbers. Use inverse operations to check that your answers make sense.

a) 40 ÷ [   ] = 8   **b)** 3 × [   ] = 27   **c)** [   ] ÷ 9 = 5

d) 360 ÷ [   ] = 40   **e)** 50 × [   ] = 3500   **f)** 1200 ÷ [   ] = 30

Unit 14: Multiply and divide numbers mentally, drawing upon known facts

1. Double each number.

    a) 46 _____

    b) 39 _____

2. Halve each number.

    a) 84 _____

    b) 98 _____

3. Use related facts to work these out.

    a) $270 \div 9 =$ _____

    b) $20 \times 800 =$ _____

    c) $3500 \div 70 =$ _____

4. Write the missing numbers in the boxes.

    a) $48 \div \boxed{} = 8$ **b)** $3600 \div \boxed{} = 90$

    c) $5 \times \boxed{} = 55$ **d)** $30 \times \boxed{} = 2100$

Unit 15: Multiply and divide whole numbers and those involving decimals by 10, 100 and 1000

1. Work out the outputs from these function machines for the given inputs.

a) 3850, 1234, 181, 99, 4.5

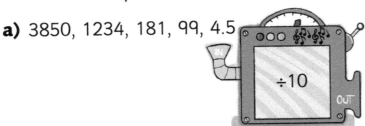

÷10

_____

b) 76, 317, 450, 56.7, 1.87

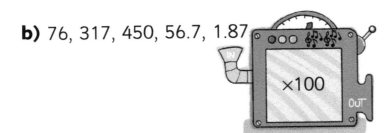

×100

_____

c) 89400, 2860, 3867, 72

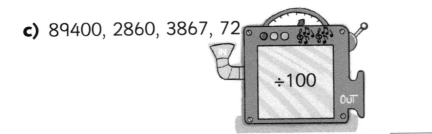

÷100

_____

2. Fill in the missing numbers to make these calculations correct.

a) 4576 ÷ ☐ = 45.76

b) 386.6 × ☐ = 3866

c) 1.241 × ☐ = 1241

d) 72 500 ÷ ☐ = 72.5

3. Complete the spider diagram.

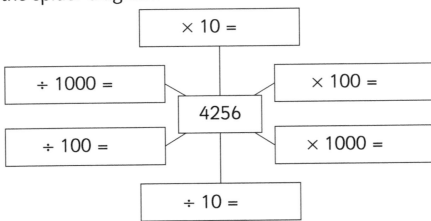

× 10 =

÷ 1000 =

× 100 =

4256

÷ 100 =

× 1000 =

÷ 10 =

Unit 15: Multiply and divide whole numbers and those involving decimals by 10, 100 and 1000

1. a) 296 × 100 = _____

b) 8570 ÷ 100 = _____

c) 3958 ÷ 1000 = _____

d) 63.4 × 10 = _____

e) 32 ÷ 10 = _____

f) 376 ÷ 100 = _____

2. Write the correct operation and number to make these statements correct.

You will not need all of the operations.

| × 10 | × 100 | × 1000 | ÷ 10 | ÷ 100 | ÷ 1000 |

a) 4.5 ⬚ = 450

b) 4500 ⬚ = 4.5

c) 0.45 ⬚ = 4.5

d) 450 ⬚ = 4.5

3. Fill in the missing number to make this correct.

⬚ ÷ 100 = 38.21

Unit 16: Multiply numbers up to four digits by a one- or two-digit number using a formal written method, including long multiplication for two-digit numbers

1. Calculate the answers. Use your chosen column method.

a) 2 5 4 6
×   3

b) 5 1 9 7
×   6

c) 2 8 0 3
×   5

2. Use your answers from question 1 to work out the answers to these multiplications.

a) 2 5 4 6
×   3 0

b) 5 1 9 7
×   6 0

c) 2 8 0 3
×   5 0

3. Calculate the answers. Use your chosen column method.

a) 1 2 5 8
×   1 6

b) 2 8 0 6
×   2 5

c) 3 0 8 4
×   3 2

Unit 16: Multiply numbers up to four digits by a one- or two-digit number using a formal written method, including long multiplication for two-digit numbers

1. Use a column method to work out 264 × 8.

2. Use a column method to work out 3274 × 8.

3. Use a column method to work out 2194 × 15.

4. Use a column method to work out 6029 × 23.

Unit 17: Divide numbers up to four digits by a one-digit number using the formal written method of short division, and interpret remainders appropriately for the context

1. Spot which of these divisions **will** have a remainder.
Write 'yes' or 'no' in each box.

a) $2875 \div 5$ ⬚

b) $4531 \div 4$ ⬚

c) $4152 \div 9$ ⬚

d) $7636 \div 4$ ⬚

2. Complete these divisions. Use the bus-stop method or the repeated subtraction method.

a) $3195 \div 5$ ⬚

b) $7396 \div 4$ ⬚

c) $2856 \div 3$ ⬚

d) $8172 \div 9$ ⬚

3. Calculate the answers to these divisions. Give any remainders as whole numbers.

a) $7294 \div 5$

b) $8263 \div 4$

Unit 17: Divide numbers up to four digits by a one-digit number using the formal written method of short division, and interpret remainders appropriately for the context

Complete these divisions. Use the bus-stop method or the repeated subtraction method. Give any remainders as whole numbers.

1. $9476 \div 4$

2. $6835 \div 5$

3. $9205 \div 3$

4. $7064 \div 9$

5. Explain how you know that $8641 \div 4$ will have a remainder.

Unit 18: Recognise and use square numbers and cube numbers, and the notation for squared (^{2}) and cubed (^{3})

1. Connect each multiplication to its correct notation and name.

Calculation	Notation	Name
$3 \times 3 \times 3$	8^3	fourth square number
4×4	3^2	eighth cube number
$8 \times 8 \times 8$	4^3	third square number
$4 \times 4 \times 4$	4^2	eighth square number
3×3	8^2	third cube number
8×8	3^3	fourth cube number

2. Rewrite these multiplications, using the correct square and cube notation.

a) $5 \times 5 \times 5 =$ _____

b) $7 \times 7 =$ _____

c) $6 \times 6 =$ _____

d) $9 \times 9 \times 9 =$ _____

3. Calculate these square and cube numbers.

a) $5 \times 5 =$ _____

b) $2 \times 2 \times 2 =$ _____

c) $10^3 =$ _____

d) $9^2 =$ _____

e) $1^3 =$ _____

f) $5^3 =$ _____

4. Write these numbers in numerals.

a) the eleventh square number _____

b) the third cube number _____

c) the first square number _____

d) the tenth cube number _____

Unit 18: Recognise and use square numbers and cube numbers, and the notation for squared (²) and cubed (³)

1. Draw the fourth square number on this grid.

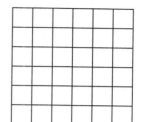

2. Rewrite these multiplications, using the correct square and cube notation.

a) $11 \times 11 \times 11 = $ _____

b) $12 \times 12 = $ _____

3. Write these as a multiplication then work out the answer.

a) $6^2 = $ _____

$= $ _____

b) $2^3 = $ _____

$= $ _____

4. Write these numbers in numerals.

a) the seventh square number   _____

b) the first cube number   _____

c) 8^2 _____

d) 4^3 _____

5. Write the square numbers from this list in the square. Write the cube numbers in the cube. **Two** numbers will appear in both the square and in the cube.

1   4   8   9   16   25   27   64   100   1000

square numbers

cube numbers

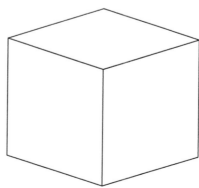

Unit 19: Solve problems involving multiplication and division, including using their knowledge of factors and multiples, squares and cubes

1. A sport club is deciding how many children to include in their club. They want to be able to split the groups into as many different team sizes as possible with no one left out.

Complete the table to show which size of teams can be made from each group size.

Draw a tick (✓) for yes and a cross (✗) for no.
The first row has been done for you.

Group size		Team size										
	2	3	4	5	6	7	8	9	10	11	12
20	✓	✗	✓	✓	✗	✗	✗	✓	✗	✗	✗
24											
30											
36											
40											

2. A laptop costs £475. A school needs to buy 25.
What is the total cost of the laptops?

_____

3. Four friends are going on holiday. The total cost is £1144.
They share the cost equally. How much does each person pay?

_____

_____

Unit 19: Solve problems involving multiplication and division, including using their knowledge of factors and multiples, squares and cubes

1. a) How many unit cubes are in this 5 cm cube?

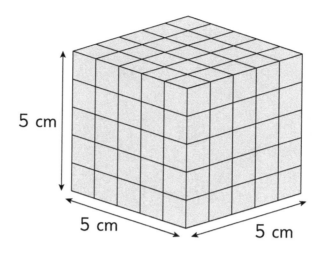

5 cm

5 cm   5 cm

b) Write the calculation in index notation. _____

2. Five people carriers, each carrying seven children, were used to transport members of a gym club to a competition. There were four children in each team.

How many teams of four children and how many reserves were taken to the competition?

_____

3. A school bought nine new bookcases. The total cost was £684. If each bookcase cost the same amount, what was the cost of one bookcase?

_____

4. Cans are packed in boxes of 24. How many cans are there in 216 boxes?

_____

Unit 20: Solve problems involving addition, subtraction, multiplication and division and a combination of these, including understanding the meaning of the equals sign

1. Write the missing operations in these calculations.

a) 24 ☐ 3 = 4 ☐ 2

b) 36 ☐ 24 = 3 ☐ 4

c) 8 ☐ 9 = 80 ☐ 8

d) (5 ☐ 6) ☐ 6 = 20 ☐ 4

2. Pair up the calculations that have the same value. Write them down.

$35 \div 7$ $(40 \div 5) + 2$ $(5 \times 5) - 15$

$99 \div 11$ $(24 \div 8) + 2$ $13 - (12 \div 3)$

_____ = _____

_____ = _____

_____ = _____

3. Solve these word problems. **You must show your working**.

a) Richie the potter sells the vases that he makes. He charges £16 for a small vase and £24 for a large vase. He sells 25 small vases and 16 large vases. It cost him £218 to make the vases. Calculate his profit (the amount of money that he makes).

£24 £16

_____

b) Last month Chris worked for 152 hours at £14 an hour. Dave worked for 139 hours and was paid £17 an hour. How much more did Dave earn than Chris?

_____

Unit 20: Solve problems involving addition, subtraction, multiplication and division and a combination of these, including understanding the meaning of the equals sign

1. Write the missing numbers in the boxes to make these number statements correct.

a) $40 - \boxed{} = 8 \times 3$

b) $(10 \times 6) - 40 = \boxed{} \times 4$

2. Write the correct operations in the boxes to complete these number statements.

a) $32 \boxed{} 4 = 22 \boxed{} 14$

b) $(6 \times 8) \boxed{} 12 = (5 \boxed{} 2) - 6$

3. What numbers could be missing?

$100 - \boxed{} - \boxed{} = 56$

4. The table shows some 2016 world population figures.

Country	Population
Iceland	336 060
Malta	429 344
Falkland Islands	2 563
Fiji	

a) The population of Fiji is approximately double that of Malta. Calculate the population of Fiji and add it to the table.

b) How many more people live in Fiji than in Iceland, Malta and the Falkland Islands combined?

Unit 21: Solve problems involving multiplication and division, including scaling by simple fractions and problems involving simple rates

1. Write the matching operations from the box next to each fraction.

÷ 5	÷ 5 × 4	÷ 4 × 5	÷ 4 × 3	÷ 2 × 3
÷ 3 × 2	× 5	× 3	÷ 3 × 4	÷ 3

a) $\frac{2}{3}$ _____

b) $\frac{1}{3}$ _____

c) $\frac{3}{4}$ _____

d) $\frac{1}{5}$ _____

e) $\frac{4}{5}$ _____

2. Choose the correct answers from this box.

7	8	9	10	12	15

a) $\frac{3}{4}$ of 12 = _____

b) $\frac{1}{5}$ of 35 = _____

c) $\frac{2}{3}$ of 12 = _____

d) $\frac{1}{2}$ of 24 = _____

e) $\frac{3}{10}$ of 50 = _____

f) $\frac{1}{6}$ of 60 = _____

3. Write under each label the cost of 1 item and of 3 items.

a)

5 for £45

1 item costs £ _____

3 items cost £ _____

b)

8 for £40

1 item costs £ _____

3 items cost £ _____

c)

10 for £70

1 item costs £ _____

3 items cost £ _____

4. Ruth has read $\frac{7}{10}$ of her book. Her book has 100 pages. How many pages has she read? _____

Unit 21: Solve problems involving multiplication and division, including scaling by simple fractions and problems involving simple rates

1. a) Which fraction will the number sentence $\boxed{\div 8}$ work out? _____

b) Which fraction will the number sentence $\boxed{\div 5 \times 3}$ work out?

_____

2. Calculate:

a) $\frac{1}{3}$ of 18 = _____

b) $\frac{3}{4}$ of 24 = _____

3. A bag of 4 oranges costs 80p. How much does one orange cost?

_____

80p

4. Six one metre sticks costs £48.

a) How much will 10 one metre sticks cost?

£ _____

b) How much will 3 one metre sticks cost?

£ _____

5. Which is more: $\frac{2}{9}$ of 180 or $\frac{2}{3}$ of 90? You must show your working.

_____

Unit 22: Identify, name and write equivalent fractions of a given fraction, represented visually, including tenths and hundredths

1. Shade the diagrams to show the equivalent fractions.

a) $\frac{1}{3} \equiv \frac{2}{6}$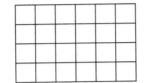

b) $\frac{1}{4} \equiv \frac{6}{24}$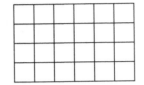

c) $\frac{1}{2} \equiv \frac{5}{10}$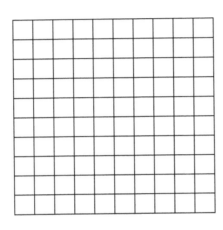

d) $\frac{3}{10} \equiv \frac{30}{100}$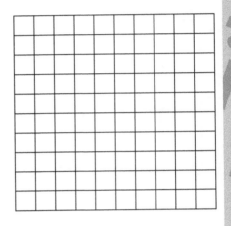

2. Write the equivalent fractions shown in these diagrams.

a) _____

b) 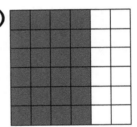 _____

3. Use doubling to continue this sequence of equivalent fractions.

a) $\frac{1}{3} \equiv \frac{2}{6} \equiv \frac{\square}{\square} \equiv \frac{\square}{\square} \equiv \frac{\square}{\square}$

b) $\frac{3}{5} \equiv \frac{\square}{\square} \equiv \frac{\square}{\square} \equiv \frac{\square}{\square} \equiv \frac{\square}{\square}$

Unit 22: Identify, name and write equivalent fractions of a given fraction, represented visually, including tenths and hundredths

1. Write the pairs of equivalent fractions.

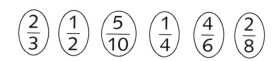

_____ ≡ _____

_____ ≡ _____

_____ ≡ _____

2. Write two equivalent fractions for each fraction.

a) $\dfrac{1}{3}$ ≡ _____ ≡ _____

b) $\dfrac{4}{5}$ ≡ _____ ≡ _____

3. Complete the pairs of equivalent fractions.

a) $\dfrac{18}{20}$ ≡ $\dfrac{\square}{10}$

b) $\dfrac{6}{10}$ ≡ $\dfrac{3}{\square}$

Unit 23: Compare and order fractions whose denominators are all multiples of the same number

1. Write each fraction in its correct box.

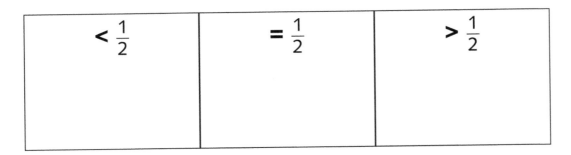

| $\dfrac{3}{6}$ | $\dfrac{4}{5}$ | $\dfrac{1}{3}$ | $\dfrac{4}{9}$ | $\dfrac{5}{10}$ | $\dfrac{3}{8}$ | $\dfrac{5}{12}$ | $\dfrac{7}{10}$ | $\dfrac{3}{10}$ | $\dfrac{3}{4}$ | $\dfrac{2}{3}$ | $\dfrac{4}{8}$ |

$< \dfrac{1}{2}$	$= \dfrac{1}{2}$	$> \dfrac{1}{2}$

2. Compare these pairs of fractions. Write one of the symbols >, < or = between them. Show your working. Use the space to change one fraction into the same denominator as the other.

a) $\dfrac{4}{5}$ ☐ $\dfrac{7}{10}$

b) $\dfrac{7}{9}$ ☐ $\dfrac{2}{3}$

c) $\dfrac{1}{3}$ ☐ $\dfrac{5}{12}$

d) $\dfrac{1}{4}$ ☐ $\dfrac{2}{8}$

3. Order these fractions, from **smallest to largest**. Use your knowledge of $\dfrac{1}{2}$.

a) $\dfrac{1}{2}, \dfrac{3}{8}, \dfrac{3}{5}$ _____

b) $\dfrac{5}{6}, \dfrac{2}{5}, \dfrac{1}{2}$ _____

4. Order these fractions, from **smallest to largest**.

a) $\dfrac{3}{4}, \dfrac{11}{12}, \dfrac{2}{3}$ _____

b) $\dfrac{3}{5}, \dfrac{7}{10}, \dfrac{5}{10}$ _____

c) $\dfrac{1}{3}, \dfrac{4}{9}, \dfrac{1}{6}$ _____

5. Oliver and Luke are reading the same book. Oliver has read $\dfrac{9}{10}$ of the book and Luke has read $\dfrac{4}{5}$. Who has read more?

Unit 23: Compare and order fractions whose denominators are all multiples of the same number

1. Write > (more than), < (less than) or = (equals) to compare each fraction to one half.

   a) $\frac{3}{5}$ ☐ $\frac{1}{2}$

   b) $\frac{6}{12}$ ☐ $\frac{1}{2}$

   c) $\frac{1}{3}$ ☐ $\frac{1}{2}$

2. Circle the **smaller** of the two fractions in each pair.

   Use equivalent fractions. Show your working.

   a) $\frac{2}{3}$　$\frac{5}{9}$

   b) $\frac{1}{4}$　$\frac{3}{8}$

   c) $\frac{5}{6}$　$\frac{9}{12}$

3. Order these fractions, from **largest to smallest**.

   a) $\frac{1}{2}, \frac{4}{5}, \frac{3}{7}$　　largest _____ smallest

   b) $\frac{3}{8}, \frac{1}{4}, \frac{1}{2}$　　largest _____ smallest

   c) $\frac{2}{3}, \frac{7}{12}, \frac{5}{6}$　　largest _____ smallest

49

Unit 24: Recognise mixed numbers and improper fractions and convert from one form to the other; write mathematical statements > 1 as mixed numbers

1. a) Shade the circles to show $2\frac{4}{5}$.

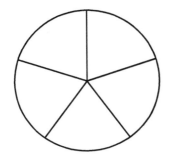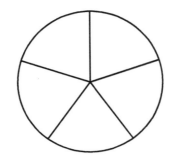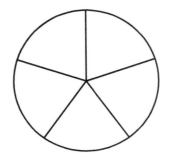

b) Write $2\frac{4}{5}$ as an improper fraction. $\dfrac{\square}{\square}$

2. Convert each mixed number to an improper fraction.

a) $3\frac{3}{10} = \dfrac{\square}{\square}$

b) $2\frac{3}{4} = \dfrac{\square}{\square}$

c) $2\frac{1}{3} = \dfrac{\square}{\square}$

3. Convert each improper fraction to a mixed number.

a) $\dfrac{24}{5} = \square\dfrac{\square}{\square}$

b) $\dfrac{39}{10} = \square\dfrac{\square}{\square}$

c) $\dfrac{7}{2} = \square\dfrac{\square}{\square}$

4. Write the answer to each addition as an improper fraction and as a mixed number.

a) $\dfrac{7}{9} + \dfrac{4}{9} = \dfrac{\square}{\square} = \square\dfrac{\square}{\square}$

b) $\dfrac{4}{5} + \dfrac{3}{5} = \dfrac{\square}{\square} = \square\dfrac{\square}{\square}$

c) $\dfrac{5}{12} + \dfrac{11}{12} = \dfrac{\square}{\square} = \square\dfrac{\square}{\square}$

Unit 24: Recognise mixed numbers and improper fractions and convert from one form to the other; write mathematical statements > 1 as mixed numbers

1. a) Write two examples of a mixed number. _____   _____

   b) Write two examples of an improper fraction. _____   _____

2. Write this value as a mixed number and as an improper fraction.

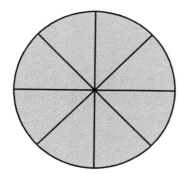 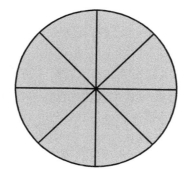 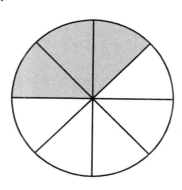

3. Convert $5\frac{2}{3}$ to an improper fraction.

$$= \frac{\square}{\square}$$

4. Convert $\frac{33}{5}$ to a mixed number.

$$= \square\frac{\square}{\square}$$

5. Add the fractions. Give your answer as an improper fraction and as a mixed number.

$$\frac{9}{11} + \frac{5}{11} = \frac{\square}{\square} = \square\frac{\square}{\square}$$

Unit 25: Add and subtract fractions with the same denominator, and denominators that are multiples of the same number

1. Is the sum more than 1, less than 1 or equal to 1? Write each addition in the correct box.

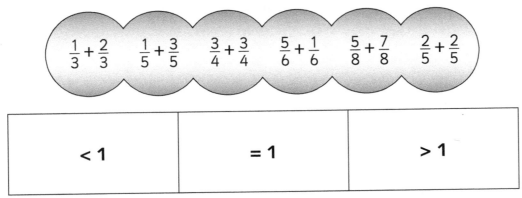

$$\frac{1}{3}+\frac{2}{3} \qquad \frac{1}{5}+\frac{3}{5} \qquad \frac{3}{4}+\frac{3}{4} \qquad \frac{5}{6}+\frac{1}{6} \qquad \frac{5}{8}+\frac{7}{8} \qquad \frac{2}{5}+\frac{2}{5}$$

< 1	= 1	> 1

2. Calculate the sum of each pair of fractions, then calculate the difference between them.

a) $\frac{3}{10}+\frac{4}{5}=\frac{3}{10}+\frac{\square}{\square}=\frac{\square}{\square}$ or $\square\frac{\square}{\square}$ $\qquad$ $\frac{4}{5}-\frac{3}{10}=\frac{\square}{\square}-\frac{\square}{\square}=\frac{\square}{\square}$ or $\frac{\square}{\square}$

b) $\frac{3}{4}+\frac{1}{2}=\frac{\square}{\square}+\frac{\square}{\square}=\frac{\square}{\square}$ or $\square\frac{\square}{\square}$ $\qquad$ $\frac{3}{4}-\frac{1}{2}=\frac{\square}{\square}-\frac{\square}{\square}=\frac{\square}{\square}$

c) $\frac{7}{8}+\frac{1}{4}=\frac{\square}{\square}+\frac{\square}{\square}=\frac{\square}{\square}$ or $\square\frac{\square}{\square}$ $\qquad$ $\frac{7}{8}-\frac{1}{4}=\frac{\square}{\square}-\frac{\square}{\square}=\frac{\square}{\square}$

d) $\frac{2}{3}+\frac{7}{12}=\frac{\square}{\square}+\frac{\square}{\square}=\frac{\square}{\square}$ or $\square\frac{\square}{\square}$ $\qquad$ $\frac{2}{3}-\frac{7}{12}=\frac{\square}{\square}-\frac{\square}{\square}=\frac{\square}{\square}$

3. Jose has eaten $\frac{2}{3}$ of a pizza and Marnie has eaten $\frac{3}{4}$ of the same size pizza.

How much more has Marnie eaten? $\frac{\square}{\square}-\frac{\square}{\square}=\frac{\square}{\square}-\frac{\square}{\square}=\frac{\square}{\square}$

4. A family are saving to go on holiday. Last month they saved $\frac{2}{5}$ of the amount and this month they saved $\frac{3}{10}$ of the amount. What fraction of the amount have they saved altogether? Show your working.

Unit 25: Add and subtract fractions with the same denominator, and denominators that are multiples of the same number

1. Write **< 1**, **> 1** or **= 1** after each addition.

a) $\frac{4}{5} + \frac{1}{5}$ ☐

b) $\frac{7}{8} + \frac{3}{8}$ ☐

c) $\frac{1}{2} + \frac{1}{4}$ ☐

2. Calculate.

a) $\frac{1}{10} + \frac{3}{5} =$ _____

b) $\frac{7}{8} - \frac{1}{4} =$ _____

c) $\frac{5}{6} - \frac{2}{3} =$ _____

3. Give your answer as a mixed number.

$\frac{11}{12} + \frac{1}{6} =$ _____

4. How much bigger than $\frac{1}{4}$ is $\frac{1}{3}$? _____

Unit 26: Multiply proper fractions and mixed numbers by whole numbers, supported by materials and diagrams

1. Calculate and rewrite any improper fraction answers as mixed numbers.

a) $3 \times \frac{1}{5} =$ _____

b) $11 \times \frac{1}{3} =$ _____

c) $\frac{1}{8} \times 5 =$ _____

2. Join the multiplications with the same answers.

A $3 \times \frac{4}{5}$

B $5 \times \frac{3}{7}$

C $3 \times \frac{7}{10}$

D $\frac{5}{7} \times 3$

E $\frac{3}{10} \times 7$

F $\frac{3}{5} \times 4$

3. Calculate and give your answers as improper fractions **and** as mixed numbers.

a) $5 \times \frac{2}{3} =$ _____

b) $8 \times \frac{4}{5} =$ _____

c) $\frac{2}{7} \times 5 =$ _____

d) $\frac{7}{10} \times 4 =$ _____

4. Calculate these multiplications by first partitioning the mixed numbers into whole and fractional parts.

a) $9 \times 1\frac{1}{2} =$ _____

b) $4\frac{1}{4} \times 3 =$ _____

c) $4\frac{3}{5} \times 2 =$ _____

5. Max ran $3\frac{1}{4}$ times around the running track every school day for a week.

How many times around the track is that altogether?

_____

Unit 26: Multiply proper fractions and mixed numbers by whole numbers, supported by materials and diagrams

1. a) $5 \times \dfrac{1}{9} =$ _____

b) $\dfrac{1}{10} \times 7 =$ _____

2. a) $2 \times \dfrac{2}{5} =$ _____

b) $\dfrac{3}{11} \times 3 =$ _____

3. Calculate and simplify your answers where possible.

a) $7 \times \dfrac{3}{4} =$ _____

b) $\dfrac{4}{5} \times 9 =$ _____

c) $\dfrac{3}{8} \times 4 =$ _____

4. $11 \times 1\dfrac{1}{2} =$ _____

5. $10 \times 2\dfrac{1}{3} =$ _____

Unit 27: Read and write decimal numbers as fractions

1. a) Label this decimal number line.

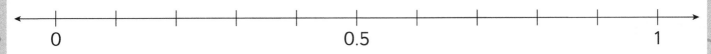

b) Label this fraction number line.

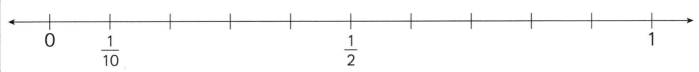

2.

| 0.1 | 0.71 | 0.5 | 0.25 | 0.05 | 0.09 | 0.2 | 0.99 |

| $\frac{2}{5}$ | $\frac{1}{4}$ | $\frac{1}{5}$ | $\frac{99}{100}$ | $\frac{1}{10}$ | $\frac{1}{2}$ | $\frac{9}{100}$ | $\frac{71}{100}$ |

a) Write the pairs of equivalent fractions and decimals. There will be one of each left over.

_____ ≡ _____   _____ ≡ _____   _____ ≡ _____

_____ ≡ _____   _____ ≡ _____   _____ ≡ _____

b) Write the correct equivalents to the decimal and the fraction that were left over.

_____ ≡ _____   _____ ≡ _____

3. Convert between decimals and fractions.

a) 0.7 = _____   **b)** 0.83 = _____   **c)** 0.6 = _____

d) $\frac{3}{10}$ = _____   **e)** $\frac{1}{5}$ = _____   **f)** $\frac{1}{100}$ = _____

4. Which is larger 0.9 or $\frac{89}{100}$? Explain how you know.

_____

Unit 27: Read and write decimal numbers as fractions

1. Write each of the values shown as a decimal and as a fraction.

a)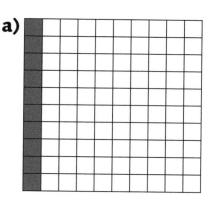

b)

c)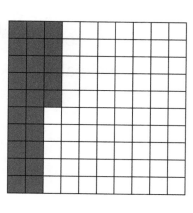

Decimal _____

Fraction _____

Decimal _____

Fraction _____

Decimal _____

Fraction _____

2. Rewrite each decimal as an equivalent fraction.

a) 0.3 = _____

b) 0.8 = _____

c) 0.23 = _____

d) 0.07 = _____

3. Write the decimal equivalent for each fraction.

a) $\frac{9}{10}$ = _____

b) $\frac{3}{5}$ = _____

c) $\frac{17}{100}$ = _____

d) $\frac{3}{100}$ = _____

4. Which is smaller 0.65 or $\frac{7}{10}$? Explain how you know.

_____

_____

Unit 28: Recognise and use thousandths and relate them to tenths, hundredths and decimal equivalents

1. Give the value of each of the decimal digits in 45.793 as a decimal, a fraction and in words.

	decimal	fraction	words
7	_____	_____	_____
9	_____	_____	_____
3	_____	_____	_____

2. Write these fractions as decimals.

a) $\frac{3}{10} =$ _____

b) $\frac{37}{100} =$ _____

c) $\frac{379}{1000} =$ _____

d) $\frac{907}{1000} =$ _____

e) $\frac{42}{1000} =$ _____

f) $\frac{29}{1000} =$ _____

g) $\frac{1}{1000} =$ _____

h) $\frac{9}{1000} =$ _____

3. Write these fractions as decimals with two decimal places.

a) $\frac{980}{1000} =$ _____

b) $\frac{360}{1000} =$ _____

4. Write these fractions as decimals with one decimal place.

a) $\frac{900}{1000} =$ _____

b) $\frac{500}{1000} =$ _____

5. Write these decimals as thousandths fractions.

a) 0.386 = _____

b) 0.215 = _____

c) 0.64 = _____

d) 0.1 = _____

6. Write these decimals and fractions in order of size, **largest to smallest**.

$\frac{43}{100}$ 0.51   0.429 $\frac{428}{1000}$

_____

Unit 28: Recognise and use thousandths and relate them to tenths, hundredths and decimal equivalents

1. What is the value of the digit **3** in each of these numbers? Give your answer as a fraction **and** in words.

a) 21.435 fraction _____ words _____

b) 5.398 fraction _____ words _____

c) 9.253 fraction _____ words _____

2. Write each of these fractions as a decimal.

a) $\dfrac{7}{1000}$ = _____

b) $\dfrac{43}{1000}$ = _____

c) $\dfrac{387}{1000}$ = _____

3. a) Write $\dfrac{750}{1000}$ as a decimal with two decimal places. _____

b) Write $\dfrac{100}{1000}$ as a decimal with one decimal place. _____

4. Write each of these decimals as a thousandths fraction.

a) 0.385 = _____

b) 0.52 = _____

c) 0.7 = _____

5. Write these decimals and fractions in order of size, **smallest to largest**.

$\dfrac{219}{1000}$ 0.2 $\dfrac{22}{100}$ 0.215

_____

Unit 29: Round decimals with two decimal places to the nearest whole number and to one decimal place

1. Connect each decimal to the whole number it rounds to.

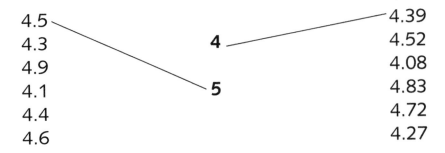

4.5
4.3
4.9
4.1
4.4
4.6

4

5

4.39
4.52
4.08
4.83
4.72
4.27

2. Round these numbers to the nearest **tenth**.

a) 5.67 _____

b) 4.32 _____

c) 6.83 _____

d) 3.19 _____

3. Use the scores on the dice to make **four** different numbers with **two decimal places**.

Round each number to the nearest whole number and to the nearest tenth. One number has been chosen for you.

	nearest whole	nearest tenth
a) 3.56	_____	_____
b)	_____	_____
c)	_____	_____
d)	_____	_____

4. Use rounding to the **nearest whole number** to get an approximate answer to these calculations.

a) 4.95 + 7.2 + 7.81 = ☐ + ☐ + ☐ = _____

b) 5.08 × 7.55 = ☐ × ☐ = _____

Unit 29: Round decimals with two decimal places to the nearest whole number and to one decimal place

1. Round these numbers to the nearest **whole number**.

a) 8.19 _____

b) 3.62 _____

c) 9.56 _____

2. Round these numbers to the nearest **tenth**.

a) 8.19 _____

b) 3.62 _____

c) 9.56 _____

3. Round these numbers to **one decimal place**.

a) 2.93 _____

b) 4.97 _____

4. Use rounding to the nearest whole number to get an approximate answer to these calculations.

a) 9.64 × 9.46 = ☐ × ☐ = _____

b) 24.09 ÷ 7.59 = ☐ ÷ ☐ = _____

5. Annie has two £10 notes. Does she have enough money to pay her bill?

Use rounding to the **nearest pound** to check.

.... £5.65

.... £9.84

.... £3.58

_____

_____

Unit 30: Read, write, order and compare numbers with up to three decimal places

1. Use the symbols < and > to compare these decimal numbers.

a) 45.62 ☐ 45.26   **b)** 12.817 ☐ 12.718

c) 17.275 ☐ 17.527   **d)** 8.643 ☐ 8.81

e) 5.6 ☐ 5.555   **f)** 6.7 ☐ 6.911

2. Order these decimal numbers, **smallest to largest**.

7.82   7.813   7.789   7.8

3. Here are the results of an athletics competition.

Put the names in order: winner, second place, third place, fourth place, fifth place.

Remember that the highest jump but the shortest time wins.

High jump (metres)	
Sara	1.209
Anna	1.175
Patsy	1.08
Nadia	1.22
Lois	1.2

800 m run (minutes)	
Tom	2.54
Greg	2.501
Ivan	3.12
Mattieu	3.104
Tudor	3.21

	High jump	800 m run
winner		
second		
third		
fourth		
fifth		

Unit 30: Read, write, order and compare numbers with up to three decimal places

1. Ring the larger of the two decimals in each pair.

a) 4.506   4.499   **b)** 7.465   7.546

c) 8.12   8.211   **d)** 2.93   2.879

e) 3.6   3.586   **f)** 8.4   8.512

2. Order these numbers, **largest to smallest**.

14.39   14.5   14.345   14.49

3. Here are three lengths of rope. Order them, from shortest to longest.

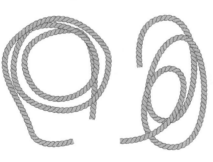 

3.45 m   3.4 m   3.445 m
   A   B   C

Unit 31: Solve problems involving number with up to three decimal places

1. Calculate these additions mentally.

a) 4.3 + 0.09 + 0.002 = _____ **b)** 8.3 + 0.6 = _____

c) 2.4 + 3.5 = _____ **d)** 6.4 + 2.8 = _____

2. Calculate these subtractions mentally.

a) 6.9 – 0.7 = _____ **b)** 9.8 – 5.7 = _____

c) 8.7 – 2.4 = _____ **d)** 9.2 – 6.5 = _____

3. Complete these calculations.

a) 8.9 + ☐ = 10 **b)** 0.39 + ☐ = 1

c) 1 – ☐ = 0.57 **d)** 10 – ☐ = 8.4

4. a) Two decimal numbers add together to equal 1. One of the numbers is 0.42.

What is the other number? _____

b) Two decimal numbers add together to equal 10. One of the numbers is 7.3.

What is the other number? _____

c) Two decimal numbers add together to equal 1. One of the numbers is 0.318.

What is the other number? _____

d) Two decimal numbers add together to equal 10. One of the numbers is 7.26.

What is the other number? _____

5. What is the number half way between 8.6 and 4.4?

```
  ←——————|——————————————————|——————————————————————————|——→
         4.4                 ?                          8.6
```

Unit 31: Solve problems involving number with up to three decimal places

6. Add these numbers. Use a written column method.

a) 2.476 + 7.849

b) 4.582 + 6.546

c) 5.62 + 4.387

d) 4.5 + 2.953

7. Subtract these numbers. Use a written column method.

a) 6.273 − 3.684

b) 7.25 − 4.287

c) 8.3 − 4.915

d) 7.5 − 3.619

8. Ian is doing a long-distance walk. He walked 6.5 km the first day, 7.23 km the next day and 6.185 km the third day.

a) What is the total distance he walked?

_____

b) How much further did he walk on the second day than on the third day?

_____

c) How much further does he need to walk to have completed 20 km?

_____

Unit 31: Solve problems involving number with up to three decimal places

1. Complete these additions.

a) $5.3 +$ ☐ $= 10$ **b)** $7.09 +$ ☐ $= 10$

2. Two decimal numbers add together to equal 1. One of the numbers is 0.25

What is the other number? _____

3. a) $7.1 + 0.05 + 0.004 =$ ☐

b) $7.2 + 0.7 =$ ☐

c) $12.8 - 9.5 =$ ☐

4. Here is the scoreboard for the triple jump.

position	length (metres)
Marty	12.245
Jonathan	12.3
Andy	12.098
Simon	12.254

Marty
Jonathan
Andy
Simon

a) Write in the table who came first, second, third and fourth.

position	name
first	
second	
third	
fourth	

b) How much **further** did Jonathan jump than Andy? _____

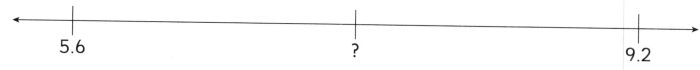

Unit 31: Solve problems involving number with up to three decimal places

5. What is the number halfway between 9.2 and 5.6?

5.6   ?   9.2

6. How much longer is 3.45 metres than 1.294 metres?

7. Complete this pyramid. Each number is the sum of the two numbers under it.

7.6

1.2   4.3

8. Diane buys these items. What change does she get from £20?

.... £4.59

.... 65p

.... £12.99

9. How much taller is Neil than Susie?

Susie 1.45 m   Neil 1.5 m

Unit 32: Recognise the per cent symbol (%) and understand that per cent relates to 'number of parts per hundred'; write percentages as a fraction with denominator 100, and as a decimal.

1. a) What percentage does the diagram show?

_____

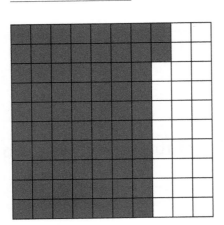

b) Shade the hundred grid to show 15%.

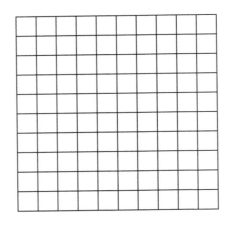

2. Change these percentages into fractions out of 100 or out of 10.

a) 37% _____

b) 70% _____

c) 60% _____

d) 1% _____

3. Change these percentages into decimals.

a) 84% _____

b) 17% _____

c) 80% _____

d) 3% _____

4. Write the matching trios of percentage, fraction and decimal.

5. Order these values, smallest to largest.

$\frac{82}{100}$ 81% $\frac{9}{100}$ 0.825

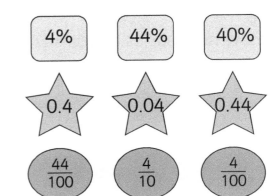

4%   44%   40%

0.4   0.04   0.44

$\frac{44}{100}$ $\frac{4}{10}$ $\frac{4}{100}$

Unit 32: Recognise the per cent symbol (%) and understand that per cent relates to 'number of parts per hundred'; write percentages as a fraction with denominator 100, and as a decimal.

1. a) What percentage does the diagram show?

_____

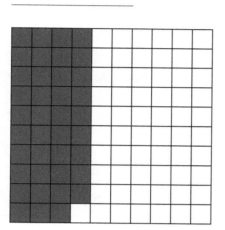

b) Shade the hundred grid to show 28%.

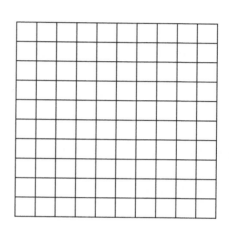

2. Write these percentages as fractions out of 100 or out of 10 and as decimals.

a) 59% = _____ = _____

b) 10% = _____ = _____

c) 6% = _____ = _____

3. Write these decimals as percentages.

a) 0.89 = ⬚ %   **b)** 0.2 = ⬚ %   **c)** 0.03 = ⬚ %

4. Write these fractions as percentages.

a) $\frac{19}{100}$ = ⬚ %   **b)** $\frac{5}{100}$ = ⬚ %   **c)** $\frac{80}{100}$ = ⬚ %

5. Order these values, largest to smallest.

0.7 $\frac{73}{100}$ 72%   0.729

_____

Unit 33: Solve problems which require knowing percentage and decimal equivalents of $\frac{1}{2}$, $\frac{1}{4}$, $\frac{1}{5}$, $\frac{2}{5}$, $\frac{4}{5}$ and those fractions with a denominator of a multiple of 10 or 25

1. Draw lines to connect the fraction to its equivalent percentage.

2. Here are Martha's subject scores.

subject	score	percentage
Maths	41 out of 50	
English	19 out of 25	
Art	8 out of 10	
Science	15 out of 20	
DT	3 out of 5	

a) Fill in the last column of the table. Write each score as a percentage.

b) Write the **subjects** in order, highest score to lowest score.

_____

3. There are 25 children in the class and 11 are boys. What is the **percentage** of boys in the class?

Unit 33: Solve problems which require knowing percentage and decimal equivalents of $\frac{1}{2}$, $\frac{1}{4}$, $\frac{1}{5}$, $\frac{2}{5}$, $\frac{4}{5}$ and those fractions with a denominator of a multiple of 10 or 25

1. Write the fraction equivalent for each percentage.

a) 50% _____

b) 25% _____

c) 70% _____

2. Write the percentage equivalent for each fraction.

a) $\frac{1}{10}$ _____

b) $\frac{3}{5}$ _____

c) $\frac{3}{4}$ _____

3. James scored thirty-eight out of fifty in a test.

What is his score as a percentage?

_____

4. Nine out of every ten children in a school are right-handed.
What percentage of children in the school are right-handed?

_____

5. Last Saturday 7 out of the 25 cars in the car park were red.
What percentage of the cars were red?

_____

Unit 34: Convert between different units of metric measure (for example, kilometre and metre; centimetre and metre; centimetre and millimetre; gram and kilogram; litre and millilitre)

1. Complete the tables.

kilograms	grams
1	1000
	2000
5	
	500
3.5	
	5500
0.4	
	250

metres	centimetres
1	100
2	
	500
2.5	
	450
7.5	
	10
0.8	

2. Choose numbers from the box to make the statements true.

3	30	300	3000

a) [ ] cm = [ ] m

b) [ ] ml = [ ] litres

c) [ ] mm = [ ] cm

d) [ ] km = [ ] m

3. Write × 10, ÷ 10, × 100, ÷ 100, × 1000 or ÷ 1000 in each arrow

a) cm  metres

b) km  metres

c) ml 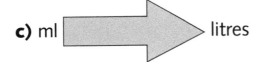 litres

d) mm 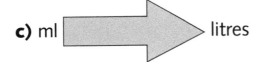 cm

4. Convert each measure.

a) 6000 g = [ ] kg

b) 40 mm = [ ] cm

c) 3.5 km = [ ] metres

d) 750 cm = [ ] m

e) 0.5 kg = [ ] grams

f) 7.5 cm = [ ] mm

g) 0.2 metres = [ ] cm

h) 600 ml = [ ] litres

Unit 34: Convert between different units of metric measure (for example, kilometre and metre; centimetre and metre; centimetre and millimetre; gram and kilogram; litre and millilitre)

1. Complete the table of equivalents.

litres	ml
1	1000
	2000
0.5	
4	
	4500
0.25	
	750

2. Complete each conversion.

a) ☐ cm = 1 metre

b) 1 km = ☐ metres

c) ☐ mm = 1 cm

d) ☐ g = 1 kg

3. Write the function to convert grams to kg.

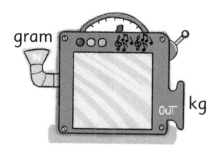
gram — kg

4. Convert each measure.

a) 600 cm = ☐ metres

b) 5000 ml = ☐ litres

c) 2.5 kg = ☐ grams

d) 35 mm = ☐ cm

e) 3600 m = ☐ km

f) 70 cm = ☐ metres

Unit 35: Understand and use approximate equivalences between metric units and common imperial units such as inches, pounds and pints

1. Write these units of measure in the correct place in the Carroll diagram below.

mile   foot   pound   litre   gram   ounce   kilometre
metre   gallon   inch   centimetre   pint   millilitre   kilogram

	length	mass	capacity
imperial			
metric			

2. 5 miles = 8 km

Complete the equivalents.

a) 10 miles = [ ] km

b) 24 km = [ ] miles

c) 50 miles = [ ] km

d) 400 km = [ ] miles

e) The journey to a French camp-site is 320 km.

How many miles is that? _____

3. a) 1 pound = 0.45 kg.

How many kilograms is 10 pounds? _____

b) 1 litre = $1\frac{3}{4}$ pints. How many pints is 4 litres? _____

4. 1 ounce = 28 g and 16 ounces = 1 pound.

How many grams = 1 pound? _____

5. 1 foot = 30 cm and 1 inch is 2.5 cm.

Marie's mum is 5 feet and 6 inches tall.

How tall is she in metres and centimetres? _____

Unit 35: Understand and use approximate equivalences between metric units and common imperial units such as inches, pounds and pints

1 Write these measures in the metric or the imperial box.

pint   kilogram   millilitre   mile   pound   gram

metric	imperial

2 a) 1 fluid ounce = 30 ml

Complete the conversion table.

fluid ounce	ml
1	
2	
5	
10	
20	
50	
100	

b) Use the table to work out these equivalents.

i) 4 fl ounces = ⬚ ml

ii) 15 fl ounces = ⬚ ml

iii) 90 ml = ⬚ fl ounces

iv) 330 ml = ⬚ fl ounces

3. 1 pound = 0.45 kg and 1 kg = 2.2 pounds

A newborn baby boy weighs 3.5 kg. His mother weighed $7\frac{1}{2}$ pounds as a newborn. Who was heavier at the time of their birth, the baby boy or his mother? Show how you know.

Unit 36: Measure and calculate the perimeter of composite rectilinear shapes in centimetres and metres

1. Explain what the **perimeter** of a shape is.

_____

2. Calculate the perimeter of each shape. Write each as an addition and as a multiplication.

Each square is 1 cm by 1 cm.

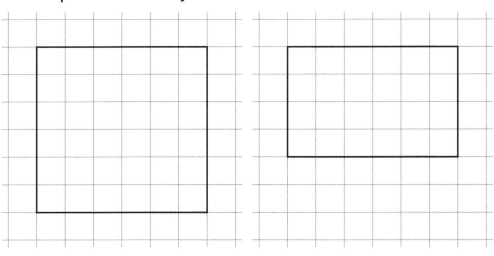

a) P =   **b)** P =

3. Calculate the perimeter of each shape.

a) P = _____   **b)** P = _____

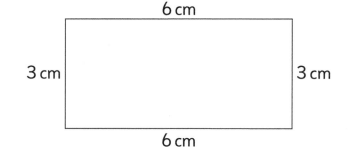

4. Work out the perimeter of this shape.   P = _____

Unit 36: Measure and calculate the perimeter of composite rectilinear shapes in centimetres and metres

1. Calculate the perimeter of each shape.

Write each as an addition and by using multiplication.

a)

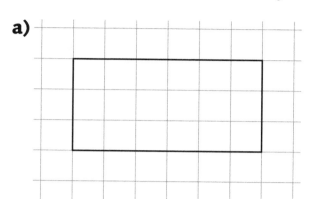

b)

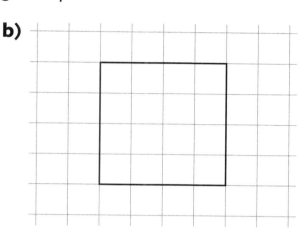

Perimeter = _____

Perimeter = _____

2. A rectangular flowerbed is 3 m by 7 m.

What is the perimeter of the flowerbed?

Perimeter = _____

3. Calculate the perimeter of this shape.

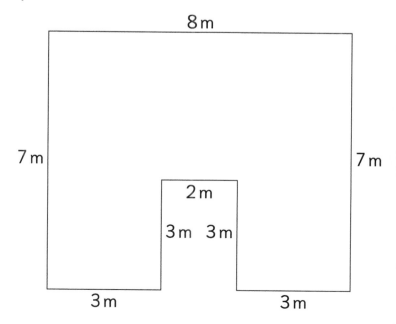

Perimeter = _____

Unit 37: Calculate and compare the area of rectangles (including squares), including using standard units, square centimetres (cm²)and square metres (m²), and estimate the area of irregular shapes

1. Work out the area of each shape.

The shapes are not drawn to scale. Use index notation in your answers.

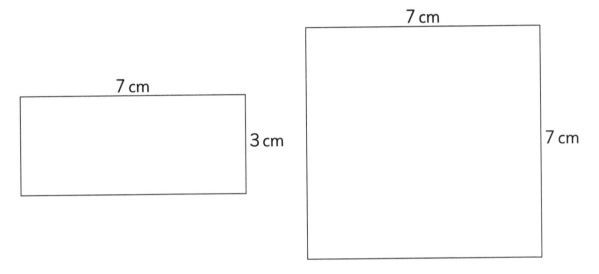

a) Area = _____

b) Area = _____

2. Two farmers are comparing the areas of their barns. Farmer Brown has a square barn 8 m long. Farmer Holland has a rectangular barn 6 m wide and 9 m long.

Whose barn has the larger area? Show how you know.

_____

_____

3. Estimate the area of this circle. The area of each square is 1 cm².

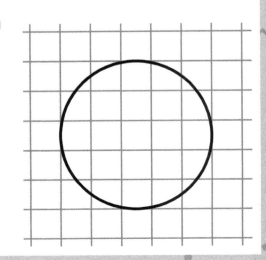

Area = _____ cm²

Unit 37: Calculate and compare the area of rectangles (including squares), including using standard units, square centimetres (cm²) and square metres (m²), and estimate the area of irregular shapes

1. Work out the area of this **square**. It is **not** drawn full size.

Use index notation in your answer.

9 cm

Area = _____

2. Work out the areas of this rectangle and this square. They are **not** drawn to size.

Use index notation in your answer.

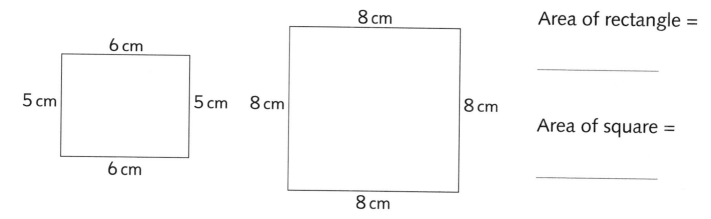

6 cm

5 cm   5 cm

6 cm

8 cm

8 cm   8 cm

8 cm

Area of rectangle =

_____

Area of square =

_____

3. Estimate the area of this shape.

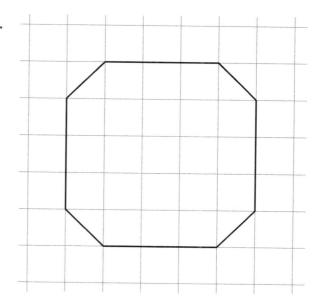

Area = _____

Unit 38: Estimate volume and capacity

1. Match the shapes that have the same volume by drawing lines to connect them.

a)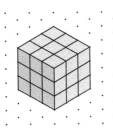

b)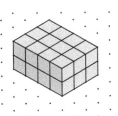

c)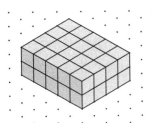

d)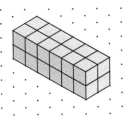

e)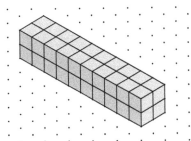

f)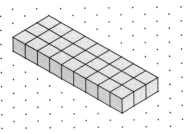

2. a) Draw an arrow on container A to show 250 ml.

  b) What is the volume of liquid in container B?

  _____

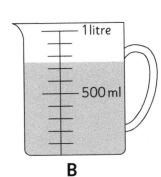

A

B

3. The amount of liquid in container A is 700 ml.

Estimate how much liquid is in container B. _____

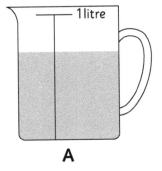

A

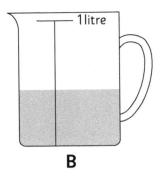

B

4. Cuboid A has a volume of 36 cm³.

What is the approximate volume of cuboid B? _____

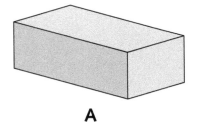

A

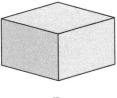

B

Unit 38: Estimate volume and capacity

1. Calculate the volume of each cuboid.

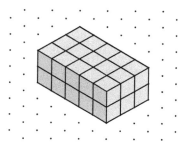

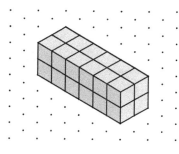

a) _____

b) _____

2. Draw an arrow on the container to show 450 ml.

3. a) What is the capacity of this container?

_____

b) What is the volume of liquid in the container?

_____

4. Estimate the volume of liquid in this container. _____

Measurement

Unit 39: Solve problems involving converting between units of time

1. Pick the correct number from the box to complete each statement.

| 20 | 21 | 15 | 26 | 29 | 30 |

a) There are [   ] days in three weeks.

b) There are [   ] days in February 2020.

c) There are [   ] weeks in six months.

d) There are [   ] minutes in $\frac{1}{4}$ hour.

e) There are [   ] seconds in $\frac{1}{3}$ of a minute.

f) There are [   ] days in June.

2. What is 210 minutes in hours and minutes? _____

3. How many days is 120 hours? _____

4. Pat's watch is 15 minutes slow. What is the actual time?

_____

5. Oliver was at his nan's house from 9:50 until 13:45.

How long did he stay there?

_____

Unit 39: Solve problems involving converting between units of time

1. Show five to six on each clock face.

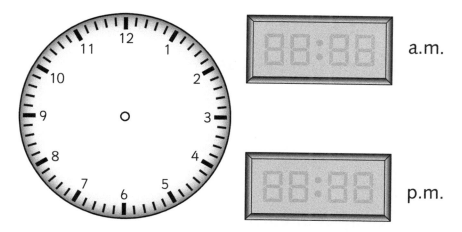

a.m.

p.m.

2. a) How many weeks is 28 days? _____

b) How many months are there in $3\frac{1}{2}$ years? _____

c) How many minutes are there in $2\frac{3}{4}$ hours? _____

3. What is 195 seconds in minutes and seconds? _____

4. Natalia's watch is 20 minutes fast. What time is it?

_____

5. School registration is at 8:55.

Lunch is at 12:15.

How long is the time between registration and lunch?

_____

Unit 40: Use all four operations to solve problems involving measure using decimal notation, including scaling

1. Write the pairs of equivalent capacities.

| 1.45 litres | 1.405 litres | 1.4 litres | 0.4 litres | 0.45 litres |

$\frac{2}{5}$ litre   1400 ml   450 ml   1 litre 450 ml   1405 ml

_____ = _____   _____ = _____

_____ = _____   _____ = _____

_____ = _____

2. Write these lengths in order, **shortest to longest**.

$\frac{3}{4}$ m   0.72 m   1 m   70 cm   74 cm

_____

3. Alice spent £1.35 and £2.15. She still has half of her money left.

How much money did she have to start with?

_____

4. At a school fair eight cakes cost £7.20.
Four of the same cakes and 2 cups of
tea costs £6.

How much does **one** cup of tea cost?

_____

5. At the cash-and-carry store a box of chocolates weighs 2.5 kg and costs £5.

a) How many 100 g bags of chocolates can be made from the box?

_____

b) The 100 g bags are sold for 40p each. How much profit is made by selling
all the 100 g bags?

_____

Unit 40: Use all four operations to solve problems involving measure using decimal notation, including scaling

6. Here are the ingredients to make 8 pancakes.

 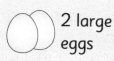 

For 8 pancakes: 120 g plain flour

2 large eggs

320 ml milk

a) How much flour is needed to make 16 pancakes? _____

b) How many eggs are needed to make 4 pancakes? _____

c) How much milk is needed to make 1 pancake? _____

d) Josie uses 8 eggs for a pancake party. How many pancakes can she make?

_____

7. Write each amount as a fraction of the unit of measure shown.

a) 250 g = _____ kg

b) 750 ml = _____ litre

c) 10 cm = _____ m

d) 600 m = _____ km

8. Write each fraction of an amount in the unit of measure shown.

a) $\frac{1}{2}$ litre = _____ ml

b) $\frac{3}{4}$ kg = _____ g

c) $\frac{1}{10}$ km = _____ m

d) $\frac{1}{5}$ m = _____ cm

e) $1\frac{7}{10}$ m = _____ cm

f) $2\frac{1}{4}$ kg = _____ g

9. Two lengths of rope are cut from a 6 m reel. One is 1.25 m long and the other is 2.9 m long. How much is left on the reel?

_____

10. Ten friends buy 2 large pizzas and 4 small pizzas. They share the cost equally. How much does each person pay?

_____

£8.50   £5.25

11. Jude makes a fruit drink out of 1 litre 500 ml orange juice, $3\frac{1}{4}$ litres of lemonade and 0.75 litres of apple juice. How many litres of fruit drink has Jude made?

_____

Unit 40: Use all four operations to solve problems involving measure using decimal notation, including scaling

1. a) How many millilitres is $\frac{1}{10}$ of a litre? _____

   b) How many centimetres is $\frac{1}{2}$ metre? _____

   c) How many metres is $\frac{3}{4}$ km? _____

   d) How many grams is $1\frac{9}{10}$ kg? _____

2. a) Write 30 cm as a fraction of 1 metre. _____

   b) Write 250 g as a fraction of 1 kg. _____

3. How many 20 cm pieces of tape can be cut from a 3 m roll?

_____

4. Here are the ingredients to make 10 large cookies.

   • 100 g sugar   • 200 g flour

   • 2 eggs   • 50 ml milk

   a) Complete the tables for sugar, flour and milk, then answer the questions.

cookies	sugar
10	100 g
5	
20	
1	
25	

cookies	flour
10	200 g
5	
20	
1	
15	

cookies	milk
10	50 ml
5	
20	
1	
	200 ml

   b) How much flour is needed to make 15 cookies? _____

   c) How much sugar is needed to make 25 cookies? _____

   d) Andi uses 200 ml of milk in this recipe.

   How many cookies did he make? _____

Unit 40: Use all four operations to solve problems involving measure using decimal notation, including scaling

5. Zoe makes a breakfast mix using 400 g of sultanas, 1.2 kg of oats and $\frac{1}{4}$ kg of mixed nuts. What is the total mass of her breakfast mix?

6. Here is a price list.

Pineapple £1.99

Mango 85p

Melon £1.25

A family buys 2 pineapples, 4 mangoes and a melon.
They pay with two £5 notes. How much change do they get?

7. Lindi is cooking a meal for 50 people. She allows 90 g of rice per person.

She buys her rice in 1.5 kg packets.
How many packets of rice does she need to buy?

8. People should drink about 2 litres of water each day to stay healthy.

How many 250 ml glasses of water is that?

Unit 41: Identify 3-D shapes, including cubes and other cuboids, from 2-D representations

1. Tick the shapes that are nets of prisms. Include cubes and cuboids.

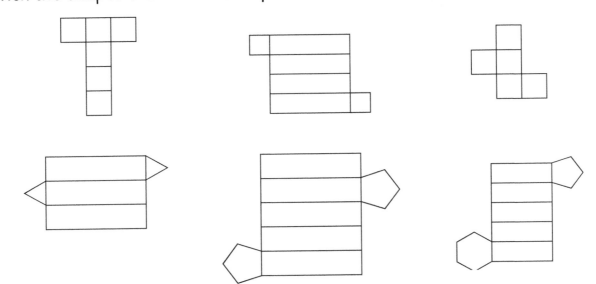

2. Complete the nets of these pyramids. The base is the shaded shape.

Write the name of the pyramid next to its net.

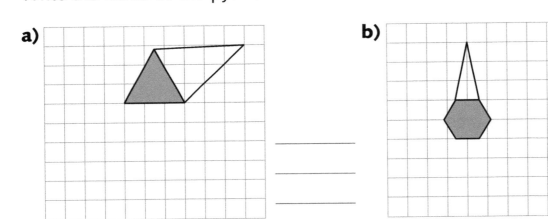

a)

b)

3. Connect the name of each 3D shape with its net.

| pentagonal-based pyramid | pentagonal prism | cylinder |

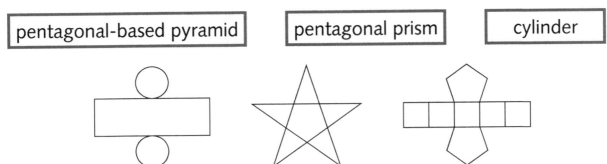

Unit 41: Identify 3-D shapes, including cubes and other cuboids, from 2-D representations

1. Complete the net for this pyramid. Write the name of the pyramid underneath.

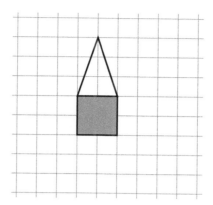

_____

2. Complete the net for this 3-D shape. The end piece is shaded.

Write the name of the shape underneath.

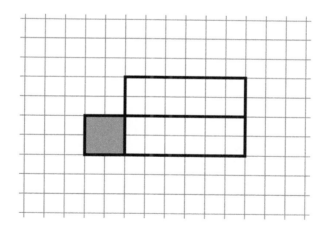

_____

3. Write the name of each 3-D shape from its 2-D net.

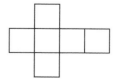 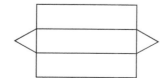

_____   _____   _____

Unit 42: Know angles are measured in degrees: estimate and compare acute, obtuse and reflex angles

1. Write acute, obtuse, reflex or right angle under each of the diagrams.

a)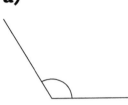

b)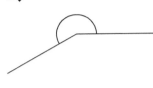

c)

d)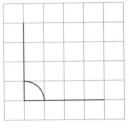

_____

_____

_____

e)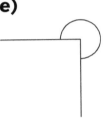

f)

g)

h)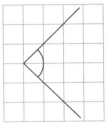

_____

_____

_____

_____

2. Label the angles in shapes below, right angle, acute angle, obtuse angle or reflex angle.

a) _____ _____

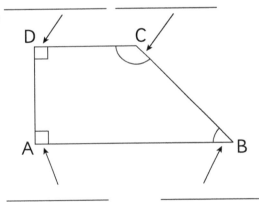

_____   _____

b) _____

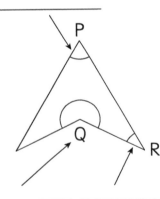

_____   _____

3. Draw the named angle on the grid.

_____

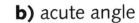

a) reflex angle   **b)** acute angle   **c)** obtuse angle

Unit 42: Know angles are measured in degrees: estimate and compare acute, obtuse and reflex angles

1. Write the angle shown in each diagram, choosing from the angles given.

| 45° | right angle | 200° | 135° |

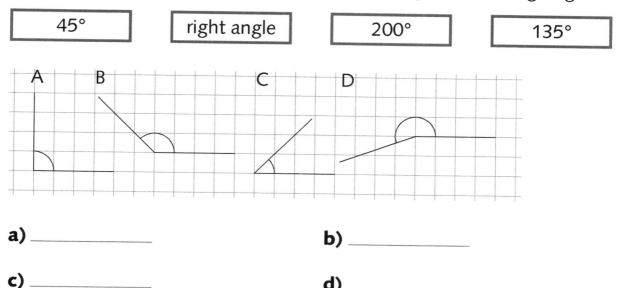

a) _____   **b)** _____

c) _____   **d)** _____

2. Label the angles in shape below, right angle, acute angle, obtuse angle or reflex angle.

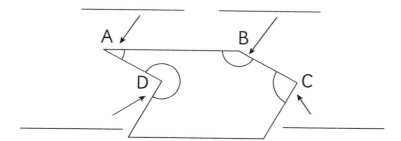

3. Draw an example of the named angle on the grid.

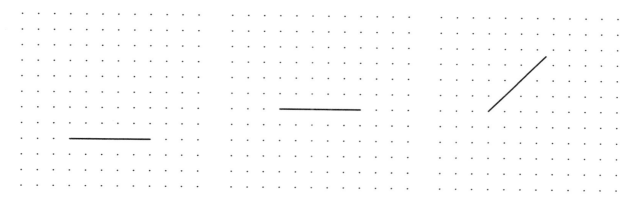

a) obtuse angle   **b)** reflex angle   **c)** right angle

Unit 43: Draw given angles, and measure them in degrees

1. Which angle is it? Circle the correct measurement for each angle.

a) 60°   120°   **b)** 35°   145°   **c)** 75°   105°   **d)** 38°   142°

2. Measure these angles to the nearest degree.

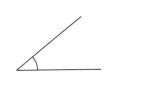

a) _____

b) _____

c) _____

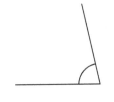

d) _____

3. Measure the angles in this shape.

A) _____

B) _____

C) _____

D) _____

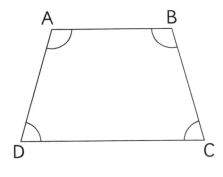

4. Draw this triangle accurately, using the baseline drawn below.

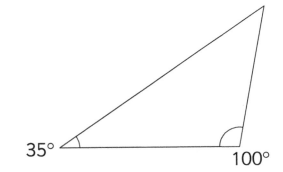

_____   35°   100°

Unit 43: Draw given angles, and measure them in degrees

1. Ring the correct measurement for each angle. Do **not** use a protractor.

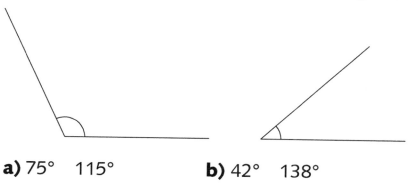

a) 75°   115°   **b)** 42°   138°

2. Measure these angles to the nearest degree.

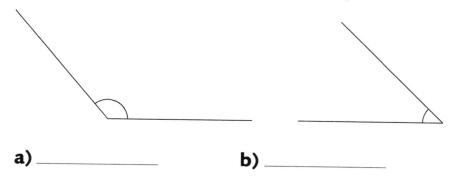

a) _____   **b)** _____

3. Draw these angles and write the size of the angles.

   a) 155°   **b)** 85°

_____   _____

4. Measure the angles in this shape.

   A = [   ]°   B = [   ]°   C = [   ]°

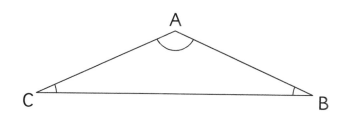

Unit 44: Identify: angles at a point and one whole turn (total 360°); angles at a point on a straight line and ½ a turn (total 180°); other multiples of 90°

1. Measure the angles on these lines. Write them down.

Do they add to the correct total?

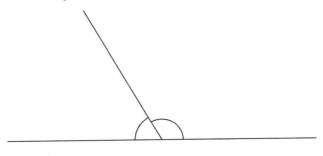

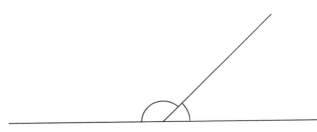

a) _____° and _____°

b) _____° and _____°

2. Calculate the missing angles.

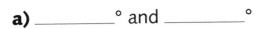

 140°

 45°

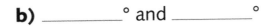 25°

a) _____

b) _____

c) _____

3. Calculate all the missing angles. You do not need to measure them.

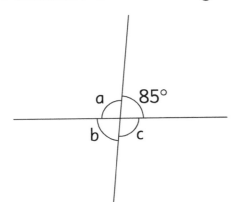

a   85°

b   c

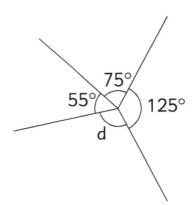

75°

55°   125°

d

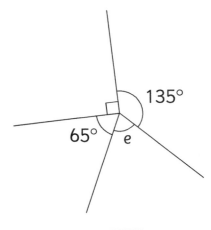

135°

65°   e

a) a = [　　　]°

b = [　　　]°

c = [　　　]°

b) d = [　　　]°

c) e = [　　　]°

Geometry – properties of shapes

Unit 44: Identify: angles at a point and one whole turn (total 360°); angles at a point on a straight line and $\frac{1}{2}$ a turn (total 180°); other multiples of 90°

1. Alice has measured these angles. How do you know that Alice has made a mistake?

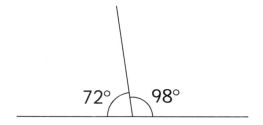

2. Work out the missing angle on this line.

$a = $ [   ] °

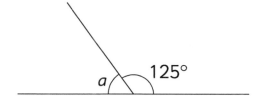

3. Calculate the size of the angle marked *b* on this line.

$b = $ [   ] °

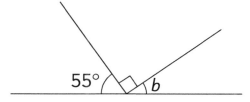

4. Calculate the angles marked *p*, *q* and *r*.

$p = $ [   ] °

$q = $ [   ] °

$r = $ [   ] °

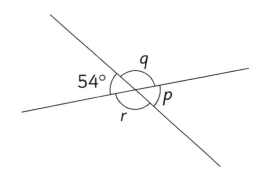

5. What is the size of the angle marked X?

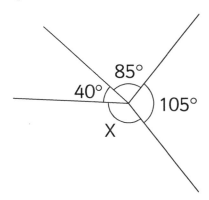

Unit 45: Use the properties of rectangles to deduce related facts and find missing lengths and angles

1. Draw a rectangle. Mark in the right angles and equal sides. Draw its diagonals and show the equal angles at the centre.

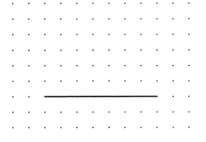

2. a) Label the other sides of the rectangle with the correct sizes.

    b) Write in the size of the angles marked *a*, *b* and *c*.

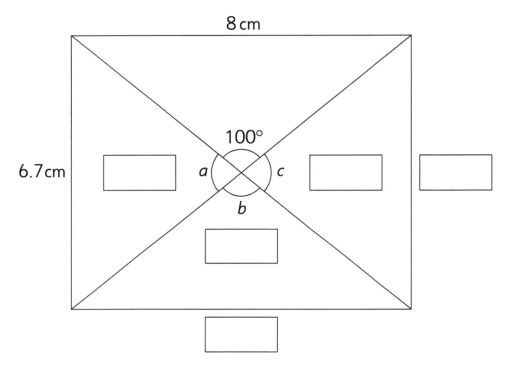

8 cm

6.7 cm

100°

a

b

c

3. A rectangle has a perimeter of 70 cm. Its length is 20 cm. How wide is it?

_____

4. Another rectangle has an area of 30 cm². Its width is 3 cm, what is it length?

_____

Unit 45: Use the properties of rectangles to deduce related facts and find missing lengths and angles

1. Tick (✓) all the statements that are properties of a rectangle.

Opposite sides are parallel. ☐ Opposite sides are equal. ☐

Diagonals bisect at right angles. ☐ Has acute and obtuse angles. ☐

All sides are of equal length. ☐ All angles are 90°. ☐

2. a) Label the other sides of the rectangle with the correct sizes

b) Write in the size of the angles marked *d*, *e* and *f*.

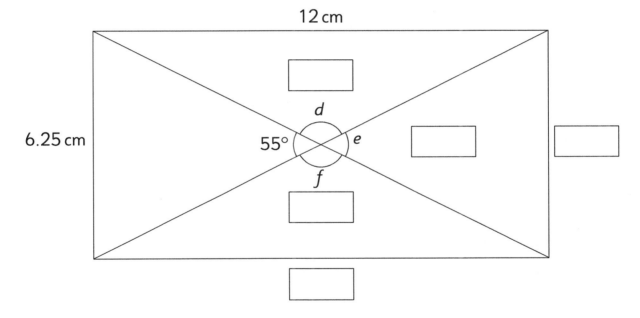

3. A rectangle has a perimeter of 100 cm. Its width is 30 cm. How long is it?

_____

4. Another rectangle has an area of 40 cm². Its length is 8 cm, what is its width?

_____

Unit 46: Distinguish between regular and irregular polygons based on reasoning about equal sides and angles

1. Complete the table by drawing ticks (✓) or crosses (✗) to show the properties of each shape.

shape	1 or more right angles	some or all angles are equal	more than 4 sides	1 or more pairs of parallel sides

2. Write the name of each shape in the correct place in the Carroll diagram.

| equilateral triangle | rhombus | square | kite |

	regular	irregular
parallel sides		
no parallel sides		

3. Draw the shape with these properties on the grid provided.

- Diagonally opposite angles are equal.
- Opposite sides are of equal length.
- Opposite sides are parallel.
- No right angles.

Unit 46: Distinguish between regular and irregular polygons based on reasoning about equal sides and angles

1. Write **regular** or **irregular** under each shape.

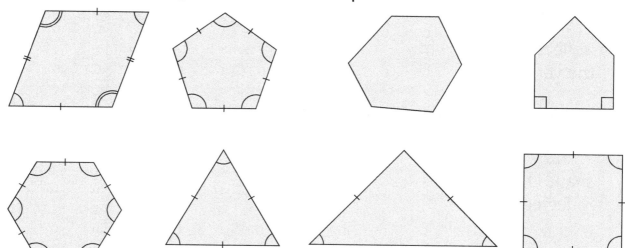

2. Show the equal sides, equal angles and the diagonals on this kite.

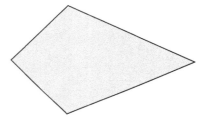

3. Write the names of the shapes in the correct place in the Carroll diagram.

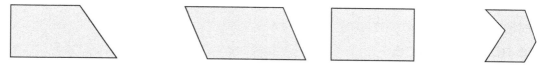

| right-angled trapezium | parallelogram | rectangle | irregular hexagon |

	90° angle(s)	**no 90° angles**
2 pairs of equal sides		
one pair of parallel sides		

4. Draw the shape with these properties on the grid provided:

- three-sided polygon
- two equal sides
- two equal angles.

Unit 47: Identify, describe and represent the position of a shape following a reflection or translation, using the appropriate language, and know that the shape has not changed

1. a) Reflect each shape in the vertical line.

b) Write the coordinates of the vertices marked X and Y when the shapes have been reflected.

X _____

Y _____

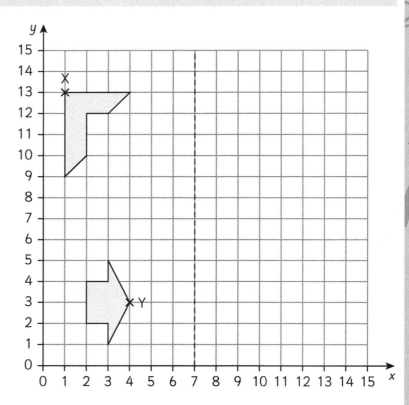

2. a) Reflect the shapes in the horizontal line.

b) Write the coordinates of the vertices marked P and Q when the shapes have been reflected.

P _____

Q _____

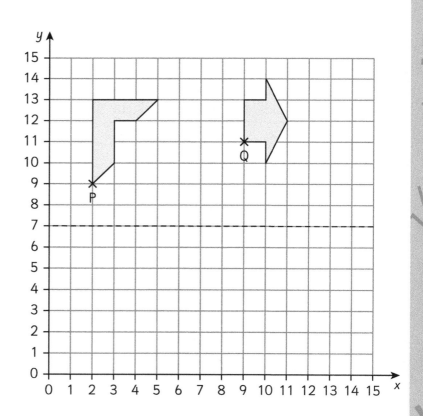

Unit 47: Identify, describe and represent the position of a shape following a reflection or translation, using the appropriate language, and know that the shape has not changed

3. a) Translate (move) shape A five squares to the right, four squares up. Label it B.

b) Translate shape A three squares to the left, two squares down. Label it C.

c) Translate shape A three squares to the left, two squares up Label it D.

d) Translate shape A two squares to the right, five squares down. Label it E.

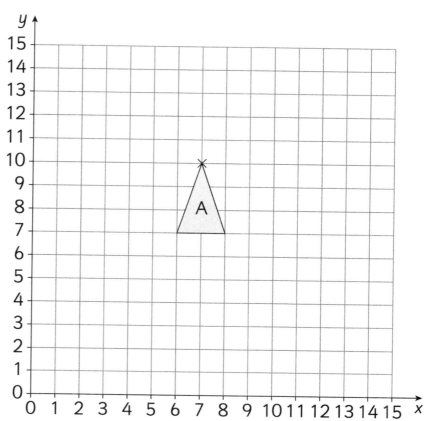

4. a) Describe the translation (movement) in Question 3 from shape B back to A.

_____

b) Describe the translation from shape C back to A.

_____

c) Describe the translation from shape B to C.

_____

d) Describe the translation from shape D to E.

_____

5. Write the new coordinates for the vertex marked X on A in the translated shapes.

B (,   )   C (,   )   D (,   )   E (,   )

Unit 47: Identify, describe and represent the position of a shape following a reflection or translation, using the appropriate language, and know that the shape has not changed

1. Reflect the shape in the line of reflection.

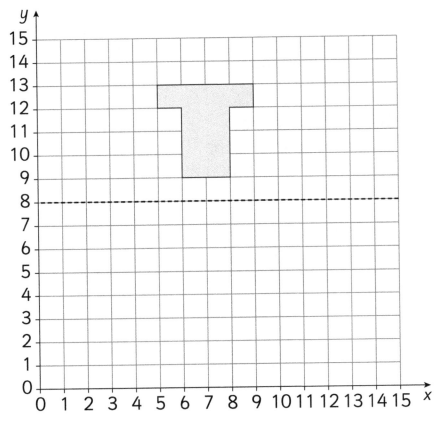

2. One shape is the reflection of the other.

Draw in the line of reflection. **Use a ruler**.

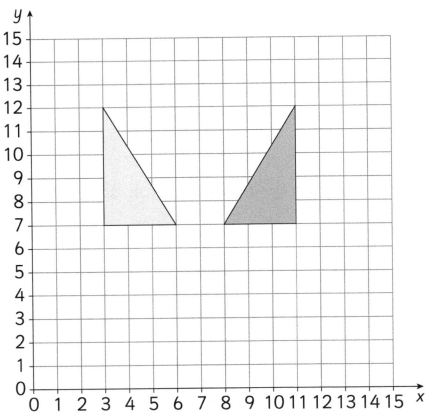

Unit 47: Identify, describe and represent the position of a shape following a reflection or translation, using the appropriate language, and know that the shape has not changed

3. a) Translate shape A three to the right, six down. Label it B.

b) Translate shape A four to the left, two up. Label it C.

c) Write the coordinates of the marked point on the translations.

B (,   )

C (,   )

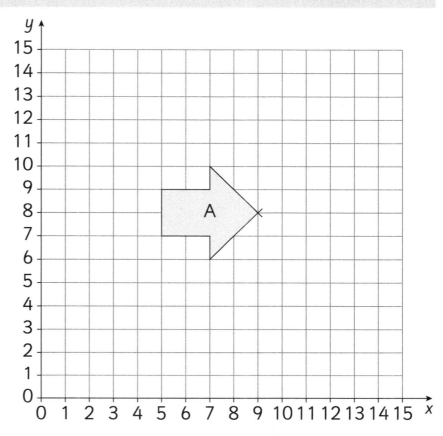

4. a) Describe the translation of P to Q.

_____

b) Describe the translation of P to R.

_____

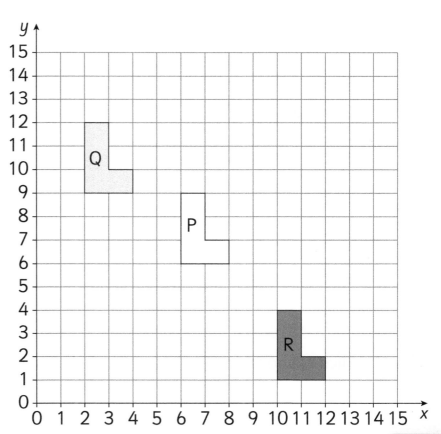

Unit 48: Solve comparison, sum and difference problems using information presented in a line graph

1. You can use this graph to convert between inches and centimetres.

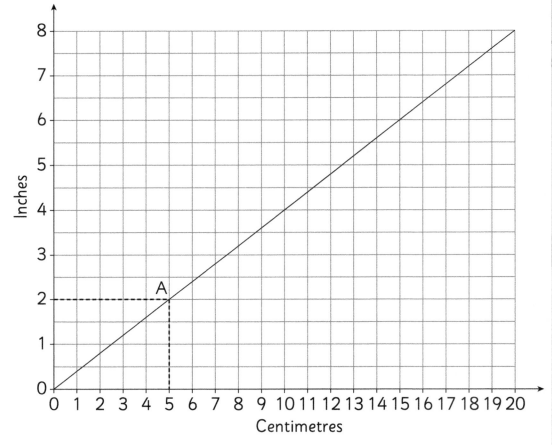

a) What does point A show? _____ inches = _____ cm

Now use the graph to convert these lengths.

b) 6 inches = _____ cm   **c)** 10 cm = _____ inches

d) 17.5 cm = _____ inches

2. Use the information in the graph to work these out.

a) 10 inches = _____ cm   **b)** 30 cm = _____ inches

3. Use the information in the graph to answer this question.

a) Which is longer, 4 inches or 11 cm? Show how you know.

_____

b) Which is shorter 11 inches or 29 cm? Show how you know.

_____

Unit 48: Solve comparison, sum and difference problems using information presented in a line graph

4. Class 5 have been recording the growth of a sunflower plant. Here are the results.

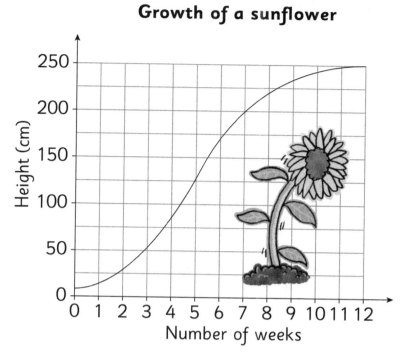

Growth of a sunflower

a) How tall is the sunflower plant after 3 weeks of growth?

_____

b) How many weeks does it take for the plant to reach 200 cm?

_____

c) Approximately how many centimetres tall is the plant after 4 weeks?

_____

d) Complete this sentence.

The plant reaches 150 cm between week _____ and week

_____ .

e) At how many weeks does the plant stop growing? _____
Explain how you know.

_____

f) Does the plant grow faster in weeks 1–6 or in weeks 6–12? _____
Explain how the graph shows this.

_____

Statistics

Unit 48: Solve comparison, sum and difference problems using information presented in a line graph

1. Use this graph to convert between miles and kilometres.

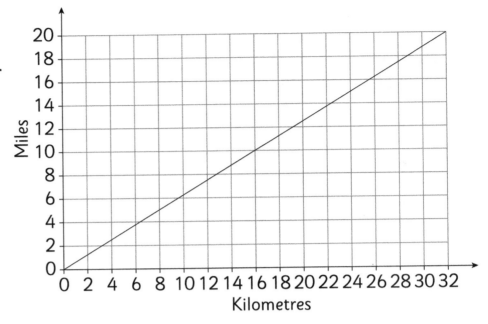

a) 5 miles = _____ km

b) 24 km = _____ miles

c) 12 miles is approximately _____ km.

d) 28 km is approximately _____ miles.

2. Use the information in the graph to work out

a) 50 miles = _____ km

b) 48 km = _____ miles

3. Use the information in the graph to explain how you know:

a) which is further, 15 miles or 23 km _____

b) which is faster, 60 miles per hour or 100 kilometres per hour. _____

_____

Unit 48: Solve comparison, sum and difference problems using information presented in a line graph

4. In a Science lesson, children observe what happens to the temperature of a hot drink when it is left to cool. They take the temperature every 5 minutes. The line graph shows the results of their experiment.

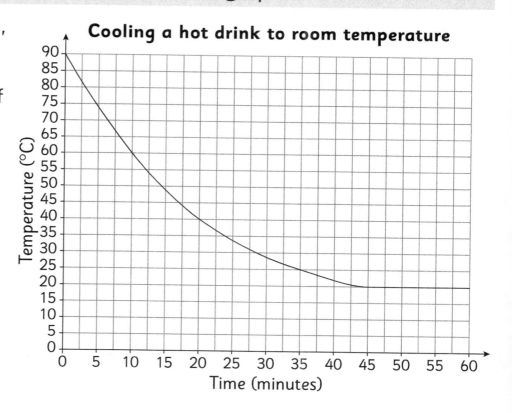

Cooling a hot drink to room temperature

a) How hot is the drink at the start of the experiment? _____

b) The drink cools to room temperature.

What is the temperature of their classroom? _____

c) How long did it take to cool to room temperature? _____

d) What was the temperature after 15 minutes? _____

e) How many minutes did it take for the temperature to reach 40 °C?

_____

f) By how many degrees did the temperature drop between 5 and 25 minutes? _____

g) Tick (✓) the time interval during which the drink decreased in temperature fastest.

☐ 0–15 minutes ☐ 15–30 minutes

☐ 30–45 minutes ☐ 45–60 minutes

Unit 49: Complete, read and interpret information in tables, including timetables

1. Here is part of a timetable for the number 10 bus between Gloucester and Cheltenham.

Gloucester to Cheltenham Route 10					
Gloucester	08:31	08:41	09:01	09:11	09:21
Hucclecote	08:47	08:57	09:17	09:27	09:37
Brockworth	08:57	09:07	09:27	09:37	09:47
Shurdington	09:04	09:14	09:34	09:44	09:54
Cheltenham	09:22	09:32	09:52	10:02	10:12

a) How long does it take to get from Gloucester to Cheltenham on the number 10 bus? _____

b) How long does it take to travel between Brockworth and Shurdington?

_____

c) Between which two stops is the longest part of the journey?

_____

d) Peter lives in Brockworth. He needs to get into Cheltenham by 10:00. What is the latest time he can be at the bus-stop in Brockworth? _____

e) The bus stays in Cheltenham for **5** minutes, then returns to Gloucester by the same route. What time will the 09:01 from Gloucester get **back** to Gloucester? _____

2. The table shows the languages learned by the **120** pupils in Year 7. Use the information below to complete the table.

- Each pupil only learns one language.
- Twice as many girls as boys learn French.
- 37 pupils learn Spanish.

	French	Spanish	German	total
Boys	13			
Girls		15		58

a) How many children learn German? _____

b) How many boys learn French or Spanish? _____

Unit 49: Complete, read and interpret information in tables, including timetables

1. The two-way table shows the number of pupils in Years 4–6.

a) Use the information below to complete the table.
There are 90 children altogether, 30 in each class.
There are the same number of girls as boys in Year 5.
There are 4 more boys than girls in Year 6.
There are 16 girls in Year 4.

	Year 4	Year 5	Year 6	Total
Boys				
Girls	16			
	30	30	30	90

b) How many girls are there in the three classes?

2. Here is part of a train timetable between Bristol and Plymouth.

	Bristol to Plymouth	
Bristol	13:44	14:45
Taunton	14:14	15:16
Exeter	14:40	15:43
Newton Abbot	14:59	16:03
Plymouth	15:40	16:48

a) How long does it take the **13:44** train to get from **Bristol** to **Exeter**?

_____

b) How long does it take the **14:45** train to get from **Taunton** to **Newton**

Abbot? _____

c) Which of these two trains takes the shortest time to get from Bristol to

Plymouth? _____

d) The **14:45** train is running 15 minutes late. What time is it expected to

reach **Plymouth**? _____

Notes